A WORD TO THE WISE

RAHAB SALMON

authorHOUSE®

AuthorHouse™
1663 Liberty Drive
Bloomington, IN 47403
www.authorhouse.com
Phone: 833-262-8899

Published by AuthorHouse 08/11/2021

ISBN: 978-1-6655-3250-1 (sc)
ISBN: 978-1-6655-3249-5 (e)

Library of Congress Control Number: 2021914677

Print information available on the last page.

Scripture quotations marked KJV are from the Holy Bible, King James Version (Authorized Version). First published in 1611. Quoted from the KJV Classic Reference Bible, Copyright © 1983 by The Zondervan Corporation.

This book is printed on acid-free paper.

The Broadway

The broadway, that wide gate
that Lures you in and Binds you
in your Sin to keep you to your End

The broadway has glitter and gold
the broadway that Grips your Soul
the broadway full of sensual pleasures
the broadway that will cause you to miss Heaven

The broadway that Binds you in Chains
the broadway that Controls your Brain and
flows like Poison in your Veins, to drive you Insane

The broadway that Sucks you dry
the broadway that Satisfies your Flesh
the broadway is nothing but DEATH

Written by,
Rahab Salmon

Thank you for choosing to ride the quiet storm your wait time is approximately forty-five minutes. This is a roller coaster ride of highs, lows, twist, turns, questions and answers that will jar your emotions and stir your soul. Step right up, choose a seat, fasten your seat belt and read the sign as you go through the tunnel. (You won't exit the same way you entered) Holy, holy, holy is the Lord of Host, God is Holy. God is flawless and spotless there is nothing of God for anyone to criticize. God is beyond scrutiny! He is El Shaddia the Mighty One able to nourish and provide. I'm talking about the one and only true and living God, sol creator, preserver, Lord and agent of all that exist or occurs. He is transcendent, eminent, almighty, eternal and everlasting. All knowing, all powerful, unstoppabe and unbeatable for he reigns supreme. God is the King of Kings, the Ancient of days, the Rock on which we stand, the ruler in all the earth, great and mighty King who can do all things. The God that gives life, the God that's greater than doctors, the God who answers prayers, the God that created the world, the God that heals, delivers and sets free. The hand through which goodness flows, the lover and owner of our soul. As you read a Word to the Wise you'll find a very structural strict standard which is Rahab

Salmon personal conviction, in which she know there are others whom may believe differently. She pass no judgment on anyone but this is nonetheless the continuation of her life out of darkness into the marvelous light. The Man of God whom God used to teach her the Word of God was patient and allowed her to gradually grow, as the spirit of God convicted her. She's fully aware that this standard of living is less favorable in today's world and she pray that no one is offended even though she know some will be. (John 8:32) And yeah shall know the truth and the truth shall make you free. I pray your freedom comes swift. (2 Corinthians 5:17) Therefore if any man be in Christ, he is a new creature: old things passed away; behold, all things are become new. Through her obedience and by faith she received her heart's desire not of herself for he is faithful that promised. When she was five years old she was asked how many children are you going to have and where are you going to live? Some place hot was always her answer and at the age of twenty-three she acted on it. She'll never forget how she sold everything in her house and jumped on a greyhound bus. Tuesday morning she applied for a Transit company and she was hired the very same day. She'd never been happier in her life. It seemed as though her dream had come true but it was the wrong man and the wrong time so she was forced to return to a empty house. You see that trial not only taught her a lesson, it revealed to her that she married him not because she loved him. But because he was a safety net allowing her to be freed from years of physical abuse in which she suffered from the hands of another man. The only words that rang in her ears were "you're just going to have baby after baby, end up on drugs or out in the streets." This was the beginning of multiple demonic spirits she battled. So she thought marriage was the answer but little did she know it would come with extreme heartache. Ladies this is from me to you don't fall for how a man praises you early in the relationship and please don't get caught up in a relationship with a person you have nothing in common with and for the love of God stop acting like you need a man more than you're next breathe or he'll have you begging like a dog for a bone. She look back at how her past relationship broke her down as she recall some of the things he would say "Don't know man want a woman with a house full of kids and by the way you not that pretty anyway, you lucky to have me because your own family don't want to be bothered with you." It's amazing now that she looks back. You see they had nothing in common he smoked, she didn't, he was a club hopper, she wasn't, his drink was dark liquor, at that time she had a natural high, she worked, he didn't, she had her own place, he didn't. Now that's a perfect example of being unequally yoked. This is a Word to the Wise if this is you; you need to reevaluate your relationship. You see she was born in sin and shaped in iniquity as the spirits begin to take root in her and grow stronger and stronger. By the age of twenty-six she had become fearless and even entertained death. Never by suicide but she always felt that she woud die by the hands of a man because of her bold lifestyle. You see she was never taught anything about life such as how to be a mother, how to be a woman, or the do's and don'ts of life. Everything she learned, she learned the hard way. No pain, no gain say's the world. She's sure somebody prayed for her though she never heard it. All she could hear was the voice of the person who stamped her brain with God don't hear the prayers of a sinner. And every time that person saw her they would say to her, you're a worldly woman and you're going to burn in hell. She never quite understood that statement because everything she had become came through their blood line. As she sat with their children who taught her how to gamble, poured her her first strong drink, introduced her to drugs, gave her her first hit and even taught her the art of cheating. Seems like to her they were all going to hell, yet she was the only one singled out. Can you imagine how painful that was? Oh and by the way they were in the adjacent room and their glass didn't have water in it. If you ask her it seemed as though every generational curse fell on her plus some magnified by ten. As she became a heartless, cold-blooded, ruthless, angry, ticking time bomb. You see she always believed in God but she never claimed to be a child of God because she knew she was a sinner. She knew she was the opposite of everything God purposed woman to be. She was in love with the world and the lifestyle thereof as she would lay in her lovers arms which was the world and cheat on God. Afterwards she would go home ball up in the middle of her bed on her knees and beg God to forgive her. Time and time again, day after day, over and over and over as a repeated nightmare. She would cry out in all honesty, Lord you know I love the world, I hunger the world, I seek the world, I desire the things of the world and it will take nothing short of you God to change me. She was lost, confused and entangled in worldliness. As she would always hear these words which were seared in her brain "all you have to do is ask God to forgive you" but something within her knew that it was more to it than just asking God for forgiveness. As a new creature in Christ; she learned the truth. Saved people don't practice sin for the Holy Ghost will keep you if you want to be kept and the Holy Ghost is also a revealer of truth. It amazes her how the secular church meaning worldly not spiritual has watered down the Word of God by having no standards and allowing anything to enter into the House of God. This is the number one statement used by the secular christian who confesses with there mouth to be saved yet in the very next breath will debate you by saying "you can't live in this world and not sin." The secular church isn't trying to stop practicing sin but the born again Christian lives not to practice sin. People of God that's where the Holy Ghost comes in, it gives you the power not to take that blow, drink that shot, fornicate or commit adultery. The Bible states in (Galatians 5:19-21) Now the works of the flesh are manifest, which are these; adultery, fornication, uncleanness, lasciviousness, idolatry, witchcraft, hatred, variances, emulations, wrath, strife, seditions, heresies, envying, murders, drunkenness, revellings, and such like: of the which I tell you before, as I have also told you in time past, that they which do such things shall not inherit the kingdom of God. If this is you you're not trying to be a servant of God instead you're a slave to sin with a form of God but you deny the power thereof because the Holy Ghost will keep you if you want to be kept. We as born again Christians should always strive to seek for perfection "Paul said I die daily." So we should seek daily to continually grow in God. The Bible states in (Romans 6:11) Likewise reckon ye also yourselves to be dead indeed unto sin, but alive unto God through Jesus Christ our Lord. People of God this is the essentials of your faith and Romans 6:11 is tailor made for those of you that say "you can't live in this world and be free from sin." The devil is a liar! That very statement is the biggest trick of the enemy and if Satan can get you to believe it as truth, you'll live your entire life freely practicing sin. Many people are in bondage because they've allowed someone to plant a demonic seed within their spirit. "Well we all are going to die of something, you only get one life you should try everything at least once and here's the big one the Bible didn't say don't drink it said don't drink that yeah shall stumble and fall that's the alcoholic's favorite justification." Gone secular church with you're bad self; right on to hell. (Proverbs 20:1) Wine is a mocker, strong drink is raging: and whoso-ever deceived thereby is not wise. Now who do you choose to believe man or the Word of God? I choose to believe (John 8:36) If the Son therefore shall make you free, ye shall be free indeed. Be not decieved you must know the Word of God for yourself because if not you will believe a lie. I was watching a religious program on television one night and I heard a false prophet say "if alcoholism is a curse in your blood line then you shouldn't drink but if it's not a curse in your blood line then it's ok for you to drink." I liken to fell out the chair. All I could hear were the words of one of my favorite preachers "Holiness is still right!" Don't you know God is coming for a church without a spot or a blemish? Are you one who's willing to take a stand for God or are you a part of this rebellious generation? If you're in bondage it's time to step off the devils turf, put down that shot glass, cigarette, get rid of that lying tongue, stop cheating, cursing, let go of jealousy, malice, clamoring, envy, animosity, hatred and unforgiveness. Yes, unforgiveness. Some of you are walking around angry and bitter with unforgiveness in your heart towards a dead person. Yes, a dead person who's grave you dropped a rose on. Now you tell me if you didn't come to a happy conclusion when they still had breathe in their body then how do you suppose you'll come to a happy conclusion now that their dead and gone. You mean to tell me you still getting drunk and crying over something you can't change? If this is you; you need to seek God for healing. People of God It's time to stop feeding those foul spirits and ask yourself why am I a puppet to sin? As you hide behind you're excuses and allow the enemy to tell you that we all fall short. This is from me to you don't give way to the trick of the adversary for your soul is at stake. You see she can recall the many times she heard "child I was something back in my day and girl you took it all the way up and you're child is going to be worse than you." Boy o boy would her blood boil and every time that curse was spoken into the atmosphere, she sent it back with the words my child will be nothing like me; Heavenly Father in the name of Jesus let not my child feet touch my iniquity. You see she was taught if you giving you better be getting cause nothings free. As they put their order in. Ladies, God didn't make you a garbage can and no it's not gold either; neither is it your personal ATM. Use it in holy matrimony as God intended that it may not become a death trap to you. Listen up it's time to stop taken down for Satan because he show know what to dangle in front of you and that spirit will work on you until it breaks you down. Let me help somebody right here. Did you know that there's a demon assigned to your life as well as a guardian angel. That demon follows you throughout your life and it tries to influence you. Yes, this is as comical as a devil on your left shoulder and a angel on your right shoulder. So this is for all you christian women whose anthem is, I'm keeping myself until God blesses me with a husband. It's been five long years (sing choir) since I've been with a man, I would rather suffer and go without for the love of God than to take down for the devil. But what she didn't know was when she said it the devil heard it. So now here he comes by way of tall, dark and handsome. Hello beautiful lady, how are you today? I've been watching you for quite sometime and I notice that there's something different about you. I work on the fifth floor so I usually only see you in the cafeteria, you always have a smile on your face and you appear to be well put together. I noticed that there's no ring on your finger and I was wondering if you're dating at this present time. She looks up with a smile (sing choir) I'm a christian woman I'm waiting on God. He laughs and responds "that's beautiful." Maybe I was sent by God can I take you to breakfast, lunch, or dinner? Now his spirit is massaging hers and here comes the carnal mind as she ponders his question. Well, it's just dinner as she accepts the invitation with the exchange of phone numbers. Look at that spirit as it slowly breaks her down and her mind begins to wonder. Hmm he smelled mighty good, you know he is my type, he got a good job with benefits, he was groomed, well dressed, soft spoken and he appears to be a gentleman. So dinner leads to him coming over and watching television just so that the two of them can get to know each other better. The relationship has grown and now she's talking on the phone to the wee hours of the morning and then he pops the big one. I want you to meet my mother he says but he's never asked about her God. Now her flesh is raring up so she tries to back off but the spirit is working on her as he begins to shower her with lavish gifts. Her conversations with her girlfriends use to be Godly but since she's become mesmerize now the three way calls are about fleshly desires. As she begins to say ladies things are getting hot between him and me. One friend responds "sister don't lower your standard and remember you told God you would wait." The other friend say's "honey child let me tell you something, you only get one life you better live it to the fullest and use it before you lose it, girl let me tell you one thing; God understands that you have needs." Do you see how quick and subtle that demonic seed was planted as the enemy used the lips of her trusted girlfriend. So now she begins to weigh the situation as she say's to herself "well maybe God did send him." Sister's let me drop you this nugget. Any man that God sends you will draw you closer to God not push you further away from God and remember God will never tempt you to sin; man is tempted by his own lust. Here comes the pity party (sing choir) I'm tired of being alone; all my friends have a husband. God what's wrong with me? Look at how the seed her trusted friend spoke into her spirit has burst as Satan begins to break her down. She was once loyal and dedicated to God but look at how easily the spirit of seduction used that man to break her down through the spirit of lust, as he waited her out with promises of lies. Yep! She finally gave in. He got what he wanted and walked away. Or she's (that is the she that's you who is) still with him. As she (that is you) count the number of children he's fathered since their (your) relationship begin, the different women she's (you've) forgiven him for and the years that have gone bye with no ring and no marriage. This is what happens when you miss God. You must learn as a true child of God to deny your flesh and wait on God because the one God has for you is right around the corner. Let's talk about the unsaved her before she became the saved me. You see I was once influenced by demonic spirits which used me to devour men, break bank accounts and destroy marriages. I was a scorned woman on a payback rampage; I was demonically inspired and bold. Every room I entered was like a candy store in which I could pick whatever flavor I desired. I was known as a terror and whatever I wanted I got, as I paraded about. Daisy dukes weren't short enough I would take the scissors and cut them up the sides, with my see through blouses and t-shirts cut down to the breast plate, along with my micro miniskirts and pipe leg jeans commando style all the way. Everything was about money; sex and riding the wave. She was raised off the words make him pay for it. So she thought that a woman's purpose was solely for satisfaction, as she would always recall that certain voice saying "never let your right hand know what your left hand is doing and remember men are no good, so dog them before they dog you." That demonic seed was planted deep within the unsaved her and it took root as she got all she could get while the getting was good. The unsaved her lived a life of abundance, yet her soul was dying slowly day by day. Let me take you further into a day in the life of the unsaved her before she became the saved me. The alarm clock would sound two pills, a shot, and a couple of pulls off a stogy, two cups of coffee and two cigarettes all before she headed to work. She would check for work complete her first half and during her lunch break, which was anywhere from two to four hours, she would go home cook dinner for her children have a shot, a beer, a few cigarettes and a nap. She would wake up to a red bull energy drink, a couple more cigarettes and a cup of coffee for the ride. she would report back to work and complete her shift, turn in her time slip, head to her car pop the trunk grab her pint and take two shots to the head, pour the rest of the strong drink into a empty water bottle and then fill it up with beer, turn on her blues and head to the juke joint to socialize till around six o'clock. Most times her drinking buddy would call her and say stop by I got some juice, that meant strong drink. After having a shot or two she would leave with one more stop to make before heading home. You see her other drinking buddy lived about a mile from her, so she would stop over and have a drink or two with her before heading home. It's now around seven thirty so that means it time for her to go home and feed her children. Once she arrived home she would burn her incense, oils and candles turn on her blues which echoed throughout the entire house and sip her wine as she served her children dinner and checked their homework. After dinner she would watch sports with her boys and help her daughter pick her outfit for school the next day. You see despite her lifestyle she had rules in her house so on school days all feet had to be off the floor by 9:00pm, TV's off by 10:00pm and only if it was a football game or a sports event did she allow the boys to stay up later. At ten O'clock she would bathe, get dressed and head out with her shot in her hand, jump in her car which was shining like a diamond, sitting on 22's with the trunk thumping. The unsaved her always had something going on and after a night out. She would head home take a pill and go on a ride. First came the itching then the laughing and the next thing she knew she was stuck. You see most people wake up in the middle of the night and drink water; she would reach on her night stand and have a shot. Ten long years she wallowed in this horrible pit, as the alarm clock would sound as if a bad dream repeating itself over and over and over again as a day in hell. She would go days without eating as she functioned off of four hours of sleep on a good night. She had the right to live her life anyway she chose and as you've read you can clearly decipher that she chose (Matthew 7:13) the wide gate, and the broad way, that leadeth to destruction and many there be which go in thereat. This is a Word to the Wise you can live your life however you so please because God is of a free will. So the choice is yours to make but understand this one thing your soul belongs to God and your choice will land you in Heaven or Hell. To those of you who have a ear to hear, a heart to believe and a mind to receive this message from heaven. If you don't turn, you will burn. What the unsaved her didn't have the right to do; was to put countless lives in jeopardy as she traveled along the streets driving a sixty-foot bus loaded to the brim. There were times when her eyes would be rolling to the back of her head and contrary to what people say opening a window didn't help. Truth be told the only thing that helped was a shot. She was bound! Sucking down her cigarettes, throwing back shots, raring back on her legs, dressed to kill, vulgar, unruly and uncontrollable. She was living Proverbs chapter seven to the fullest. (You're about to enter the first winding turn on the roller coaster.) Are you judge mental, hypocritical or self-righteous? Maybe you're the one with a double standard when it comes to matters pertaining to you and yours. This question is for all of you who feel that you're not self-righteous. Do you think the alcoholic likes to wake up in their vomit? Do you think the chain smoker enjoys being short of breathe and pulling a oxygen tank? Do you think the prostitute wants to sale herself for a blow? Do you think the thief wants to steal to support their drug addiction? Do you think people want to commit adultery? Do you really truly believe as a believer of the Word of God that a man wants to be effeminate? Do you really believe that a woman can truly believe that she is a man when she looks at her body? Or do you believe that it's a demonic spirit or maybe a mental issue? You tell me how can you make a wrong a right? Two men will never produce a child naturally neither will two women. All they can do is burn in their lust one toward another. Why be angry with me? You want to force your belief on me. You want to make me accept your lifestyle regardless of my belief. So I say to you what right do you have to force your will on me, as you reject my belief in the Word of God? Why would two men or two women adopt children and think its right to raise them believing that having two father's is natural or having two mother's is natural? Is this not deception of a impressionable mind? If you say all God wants us to do is love then why would you subject a child to your selfish Godless desire? This is a Word to the Wise the further you go sexually the more sadistic sex becomes. (The quiet storm has now increased its speed) How is it that the very ones who say that they're saved have now forgotten what God has delivered them from. As they turn and judge another instead of strengthening their brother. If you were every bound by any of these things then you know it's not the person but an evil force that impresses upon their will. Did you know that Inordinate affection promotes isolation and secrecy? If you allow a person or thing to take the place of God within your heart and God's divine order, you've chosen them as your God because at that point they've won control over you. It's as simple as that. If you yield your spirit to a inordinate affection you've chosen to put your love and adoration in the wrong place. (Romans 7:15-22) For that which I do I allow not: for what I would, that do I not; but what I hate, that do I. If then I do that which I would not, I consent unto the law that it is good. Now then it is no more I that do it, but sin that dwelleth in me. For I know that in me (that is, in my flesh,) dwelleth no good thing: for to will is present with me; but how to perform that which is good I find not. For the good that I would I do not: but the evil which I would not, that I do. Now if I do that I would not, it is no more I that do it, but sin that that dwelleth in me. I find then a law, that, when I would do good, evil is present with me. For I delight in the law of God after the inward man: But I see another law in my members, warring against the law of my mind, and bringing me into captivity to the law of sin which is in my members. If this is you and you're bound by any of these demonic spirits there's still hope for you. Remember good and evil are always at war but good men and women choose God. So stop doing things that you'll later regret and don't allow yourself to be poisoned by the world and its deceitful lust. This is a Word to the Wise let not your flesh cause you to burn turn from your wicked ways and taste and see that the Lord is good: blessed is the man that trusteth in him. Did you know that books carry spirits? Do you reach pass the Christian book and grab the romance novel that describes murder, betrayal, deceit, perversion and explicit sexuality? Did you know the more you entertain sexual spirits the more you welcome them into your life? Before you know it you'll find yourself performing some of the same sexual acts as you convince someone else to do the same, whether it be your spouse or your friend. Do you pick up your Bible like you read your newspaper, emails, magazine ect? Do you own a Bible or do you think the app on your phone counts as a Bible? How can you be a child of God without a sword? I'm not talking about toting a Bible. I'm talking about having the Word of God within the mental rolodex of your mind. Which is your true battle ground that you may be able to bring it forth via any situation or circumstance. I'm finding that many people are going to church because it's a part of their weekly routine but they have no substance. Did you know you could sit in a ministry and spiritually die? Did you know you could be bound within a dead ministry? Answer that if you will because I would love to hear your explanation for why your church house went from standing room only to at best forty members. No. All of them didn't backslide! You know the truth because you were part of the cover-up. (Hmm) Yep! That secret thing that God knows all about. This is a Word to the Wise If you don't know the Word of God you'll sit in the church house feeding from a false prophet believing that you can live like the devil and make it into Heaven. Let me say this you must have balance you can't be so spiritually minded that you're no earthly good. So I'm asking you after your deliverance then what? You got the victory over drugs, alcohol, lust, smoking, cursing, lying, cheating, stealing, jealousy, envy and the list goes on but what about that critical spirit, self-righteous spirit and religious spirit? Did you know that as a result of dogmatic preaching there are many people outside the church walls? Yes. I'm talking about church hurt there is such a thing. Many Men of God and Women of God will say church hurt is not real; it's just an excuse that members use to leave their church or to leave church all together. Ask a Woman of God who's husband had a affair and fathered a child as a result of the affair. Ask the First Lady what it feels like to hold that beautiful child not knowing that its her husbands child. Ask the Man of God who trusted his lovely wife as she went to the church house to chior rehearsal and ended up divorcing him and marrying the music director. Ask the Woman of God who's husband came out the closet and left her for deacon mustang if there's really such a thing as church hurt. Ask that husband or wife who thought their spouse was seeking deliverance from God as they became faithful to the House of God yet they were really faithful to the adultery with the Man of God or Woman of God. I'm not done yet ask the saved me who was persecuted by the church. Yes ma'am/yes sir ask once broken me. I can tell you from my very own personal experience that church hurt is real. The testiment of my life caused a great uproar you would think that a holiness ministry would have embraced such a miraculous deliverance. Instead one first lady called the other first lady who called another first lady who called another first lady. Need I say anymore but of course I will: just keep reading. Ask the multitude of members who woke up to devastating breaking news concerning the pastor they entrusted if church hurt is real. Now ask yourself have you caused someone to experience church hurt because you allowed the enemy to use you? Let me make this very clear; your church hurt is associated with the church because thats the place where the actual hurt took place. I understand your church hurt but if you'll allow me to plant this seed. The church didn't hurt you it was a demonic spirit operating through a person within the church that hurt you. As a result of your church hurt you may have chosen to leave that ministry but I speak straight into your spirit don't ever allow any person, trial, situation or circumstance to cause you to leave God! Lets take it to the altar. Men of God and Women of God if the prostitute is seeking deliverance and goes to church how do you propose she'll get delivered when the pastor is belittling, name calling, degrading and killing the person's spirit. Let me go a step further. As a Man of God or Woman of God how do you suppose God will use you to deliver the prostitute if you have bitterness in your heart for this type of individual or sin? This is a great example of how some people come to church seeking forgiveness, deliverance and salvation but instead they leave more broken. My question still stands after your deliverance then what? You think that means victory? You think that means you heaven bound? You think the battle is over and won and you have free entry into heaven? I'm serious. I'm really seriously asking you this? You think just because you ask God to forgive you after that one night stand, or lie you just told, or hangover you woke up with, or ungodly thought you had after reading something in a Word to the Wise that you didn't agree with, is all you have to do too gain excess to heaven? Well, I'm here to tell you as long as you're on this side you haven't arrived and your forgive me I'm sorry to tell you is not the password to enter into the gate you must give God a life. This is a daily walk and it's a lonesome road and few their be in passing. (Hebrews 12:13-15) And make straight paths for your feet, lest that which is lame be turned out of the way; Follow peace with all men, and holiness, without which no man shall see the Lord: Looking diligently lest any man fail of the grace of God; lest any root of bitterness springing up trouble you, and therby many be defiled;. People of God that's why deliverance is key. You can say you've been saved twenty years, thirty years, forty years and believe it or not I've heard people stand and testify that they've been saved all their life but yet you're still in danger of entering hell because you have hatred, unforgiveness, or bitterness in your heart from experiences that you suffered from your childhood, to situations you've experienced in your adult life. This is a Word to the Wise it's time to stop allowing Satan to talk to you causing you to believe a lie and end up damned. The Bible tells us (Proverbs 14:12) There is a way which seemeth right unto a man, but the end thereof are the ways of death. I'm here to tell you there's joy in the Lord, trust me when I say, you can live sin free but not if you're still entangled with the world? The unsaved me was bound as she was influenced by multiple demonic spirits. She loved her men as she was caught up in the world of fashion, expensive hand bags, exotic shoes, designer clothes, diamonds on every finger, bracelets, fancy watches, multiple gold chains, earrings for all five holes in my ears, diamond earring in my nose, long claw finger nails sparkling matching my toenails, multiple tattoos glistening and fat pockets. That's to say the lest because the unsaved her was a force to be reckoned with. Allow me to paint this picture: You pull up outside the night club as the line is already forming, the bouncer say's thirty-dollars at the door, you pay and enter. You can feel the body heat the music is off the chain and the dance floor is crowded, everyone is bumping, grinding, dropping it like its hot and slithering like a snake. You walk through find your crew and the party begins. As you consume more spirits because that's all liquor is. Oh but only if you're spiritual eye would open while you're inside that night club. Which brings me to my next thought. I don't understand how someone could be delivered from the bondage of clubbing and worldliness. Yet they can sit in a secular church where the preacher allows worldly music and worldly movies to be glorified in the House of God. Isn't that contradictory to one's deliverance? You tell me do you really believe that God sits in Heaven and laughs at your sinful ways? Do you yourself find it amusing when your Man of God or Woman of God stands in the pulpit and exposes how they saw you on live with that tight mini dress on drinking and line dancing? As the pastor say's "I saw you last night and I said she better make it to the House of God in the morning and she better be on time to lead praise and worship service." You tell me do you really believe God will choice a Man of God or Woman of God to lead his people into error or morally questionable behavior? I say to you beware and don't allow yourself to be lead astray because not every pastor is concerned with your soul being saved from a burning hell. Truth be told some are more interested in your talents. Did you know rebellion is as the sin of witchcraft? Just like when you don't do what God tells you to do you are rejecting God. If God says thou shall not, that don't mean when you don't want to or if you don't believe that way. Contrary to todays society and this so called modern day family; homo-sexuality was a sin then and homo-sexuality is a sin now. I'm just saying don't become fashioned as the world and remember God destroyed Sodom and Gomorrah. (Whatever that thought was you just had it doesn't matter because the Bible is still right) If any pastor is teaching you otherwise they themselves are not called of God they are a false prophet. I'm not condoning hate by any means, love the person, bind the spirit and remember God has the final say. The Word of God says (Psalm 37:17) For the arms of the wicked shall be broken: but the Lord upholdeth the righteous. There's one thing I know for sure God is coming back for a church without a spot or a wrinkle. So you can't live off the testimony of others. The Bible tells us that every man must work out his own soul salvation with fear and trembling. Jesus hung bleed and died for the remissions of our sins and Jesus faced the ultimate battle which was Satan! So don't you know the battle has already been won for you? Yes. God has a gift for you but you're the only one that can get your gift. What excuse do you have? Jesus sent the comforter the Holy Ghost. And if you have the Holy Ghost you have the power to keep the devil out. So turn your light on for wherever light is there can be no darkness. All we're required to do is live a life of holiness which is simple; if you allow the spirit of God and the power of his spirit to assist you. The Bible is our road map and Holy, holy holy it's a lifestyle. (That's my slogan) It's time to stop making excuses to justify your sin and take a stand and be holy, for I am holy said the Lord thy God and remember to follow peace with all men, and holiness, without which no man shall see the lord. Need I dare say that this is the fishes and loaves generation. So my question to you is. Do you serve God because you love God or for what you can get out of God? Are you serving God with a pure heart? You may be able to buy a prophecy but you can't pay your way to heaven and by the way prophecies shouldn't be sold freely received, freely given. I'm just saying why pay your way to hell when you can go for free? Don't you know God loves you? Aren't you tired of being burdened down? Are you a people pleaser? Do you spend your time on useless vain things? Are you cheating on God, by lying in your lover's arm which is the world and then turn and ask God to forgive you only to sin again? Why do you fear Satan more than God? Can you imagine being in the room watching your spouse cheat on you? Don't you know the eyes of the Lord are in every place beholding the good and the evil? Have you forgotten God is omnipotent, omniscient and omnipresent or is it that you have no fear of God? How is it that some of you act so holy in church but you live like the devil? And women what don't you understand about modest apparel, stop allowing Satan to use you by wearing alluring garments and provoking the spirit of lust. The church has become so mixed up you can't tell a christian woman from a worldly woman, when you should be able to tell the difference between a Woman of God and a worldly woman. I'm just saying, ladies go to the mirror and take a good look at yourself. (Which one are you?) I'm not putting you in hell because I have no heaven or hell to put you in. But I do won't to know, why do you shave your hair off? Is it to keep up with the world's latest fashion? I'm just asking in case you haven't been told by now, a woman's hair is her crown and glory. So ladies if you still bobbing your hair off after reading the Word of God I'm scared of you. And if you didn't know now you know holy and sexy don't go together. So pull you're blouses up and your skirts down and for God sake if your dimples are showing you need a bigger size. And while I'm at it since when did men start showing their shape, wearing to little suits and pipe leg jeans looking like bozo by the feet? The Bible says that woman should not wear that which pertains to a man. (This is my standard) So how can a Woman of God stand in the pulpit and preach with her skin tight jeans, low cut blouse, five-inch heels, finger nail polish, earrings, chains, excessive rings, bracelets and her face painted? If you're the woman I just described tell me whats the difference in how you look and the woman that looks just like you on the street corner? How can God use you to help the man who comes to the church house seeking deliverance from the spirit of lust, when you're standing in the pulpit looking worse than the woman he just left in the street? You tell me what kind of example are you setting for the impressionable and how do you figure that the worldly woman entering your edifice will see the era of her ways: when she mirrors you? This is a Word to the Wise not all preachers were called of God some where chosen because the pastor had a son or daughter to pass the ministry to. Even if the son or daughter life didn't line up and in some cases the father and son or daughter don't even have the same belief but yet and still they turn the ministry over to the child. Here we go with church hurt again just ask the many loyal bishops who knew beyond a shadow of a doubt that they were next in line only to find out upon the apostle's death that the ministry was being passed on to the Man of God's child or grandchild. Yes, that child. (The one who's diaper you changed) Well in some cases thank God for wisdom because I wouldn't pass a dynamic ministry to Man of God or Woman of God who has a track record of destroying souls. Man of God and Woman of God how can you lead two-thousand members when you've pastored over forty years and only have a hand full of members. Nope the standard is not why your church is empty. Man of God your church is empty because of you and the Woman of God. (You can close your mouth now) Oh but you said there was know such thing as church hurt Man of God and Woman Of God. I get it you just felt you had the right to bash the Man of God behind his back as you try to turn people against him. While you break bread with him, sit in his pulpit and laugh in his face like you respect him so. Yes. You tried to dig dirt from under him and turn members of the organization against him because you tried it with elder and the saved her. You spoke cruelly with evil intent and hatred in your heart toward the chosen overseer. And if that didn't seal the coffin let me add how you woud say openly across the pulpit to your members "don't go give your money to another church take care of your own church." (Checkmate) For I've found that there are pastors and first ladies that are saved yet they didn't get delivered from certain things and above that some people been saved so long that they don't realize that there in a backslidden state. The Word of God tells us to beware of wolves in sheep clothing. The life of your pastor and first lady should exemplify holiness. If the pastor or first lady of your church smoke, drink, curse or has an extra marital affair that's not of God. So you tell me why do you make excuses to justify your pastor's sin? Tell me why would you allow a Man of God or Woman of God to preach and lay hands on you when you know they don't have Holy Ghost power? This is a Word to the Wise the Holy Ghost is not a outfit you can't take it off and put it on when you so please. Are you guilty of saying, well the Pastor is human too we all make mistakes? Yes. That's true we all make mistakes but when you know better you do better. So there is no excuse for a shepherd who preaches against homosexuality, adultery, lying and stealing yet he himself or her herself is found guilty of these sins. Something is wrong with that picture to me. Don't you know that there's no compromising the Word of God. So if the shepherd of your church is living an ungodly life. Then how do you suppose that you will ever live a godly life with such an example? This is a Word to the Wise it's time to examine yourself create a check list and stop playing russian roulette with your soul. The Bible tells us that there is pleasure in sin but it's only for a season. So be not deceived for you've heard about Jesus and all his wonderous works, you know about the thirty-nine stripes and how Jesus shed his blood for us all. So whether you're saved or unsaved, whether you believe or you don't believe. The Word of God reveals to us in (2 Corinthians 5:10) For we must all appear before the judgment seat of Christ; that every one may receive the things done in his body, according to that he hath done, whether it be good or bad therefore knowing the terror of the Lord. Listen up this is a Word to the Wise there will be no time to ask for forgiveness if you die in your sin; at that moment only the reward of Hell shall be given you. I say to you heed the warning don't become as the rich man who lifted his eyes up in hell? Yes hell; there is a hell. Be not decieved don't allow any false prophet to cause you to believe that everyone is going to Heaven because that's a false truth. You will not live like the devil and enter into God's Holy Heaven. Let God be true and ever man a liar! (Luke

16:23-28) And in hell he lifted up his eyes, being in torments, and seeth Abraham afar off, and Lazarus in his bosom. And he cried and said, Father Abraham, have mercy on me, and send Lazarus, that he may dip the tip of his finger in water, and cool my tongue; for I am tormented in this flame. But Abraham said, Son, remember that thou in thy lifetime receivedest thy good things, and likewise Lazarus evil things: but now he is comforted, and thou art tormented. And beside all this, between us and you there is a great gulf fixed: so that they which would pass from hence to you cannot; neither can they pass to us, that would come from thence. Then he said, I pray thee there-fore, father, that thou wouldest send him to my father's house: For I have five brethren; that he may testify unto them, lest they also come into this place of torment. If you still don't believe there's a hell after reading it in the Word of God you are a unbelieving believer. You are as a child sitting down picking the vegetables out of their plate. This is a Word to the Wise you can't pick and choose what you're willing to believe when it comes to the Word of God you must eat the whole roll. For those of you who didn't know the biblical story concerning the rich man I'll just say to you that God didn't create hell for man hell was created for Satan and his followers. God is of a free will: God will not twist your arm to serve him but keep this in mind. As I stated before you can live your life how ever you want to live it because its your life to live but your soul belongs to God. So in your choosing: choose wisely because your reward will be Heaven or Hell. Let's take a self examination. Are you Vain? Do you worship material things such as cars, money, houses, clothes, your children, husband, mother, wife, lover, job, stars, music, and the list goes on and on? Are you the one who pulls up in front of the church house in your luxury car with your vanity plate (Blessed) and don't tithe; as you rob God. The congregation may not know your little secret but God knows that you faking the funk. The Bible says (Malachi 3:8-9) Will a man rob God? Yet ye have robbed me. But ye say, Wherein have we robbed thee? In tithes and offerings. Ye are cursed with a curse: For ye have robbed me. God doesn't need and neither does God want your scraps. You weren't a second thought to God For God so loved the world that he gave his only begotten Son and if I take it a step further Jesus laid his life down for us all. That's for all of you who say God knows I don't have any money left after I pay my bills. Allow me to enlighten you. Deceit and lying are present in the lives of those who are not the Lords. (read Acts 5:1-11) Ananias and Sapphira are the ultimate example of disobedience, greed and deceit. As they surreptitiously agreed together to lie to the Holy Ghost. Falsehood and hypocrisy were the sins in which Ananias and Sapphira were severely punished for. As the solemn word of judgment was pronounced and sudden death overtook both of them. When you enter the House of God put away all guile because the altar is a altering place you can go down to the altar dead and come away alive or you can go down to the altar alive and fall dead. (I wouldn't laugh at that) If I were you I would be very careful how I handle Gods anointed one's especially those who are filled with the baptism of the Holy Ghost. Because you're not only coming into the presence of a person you're also coming into the presence of the Holy Ghost that dwelleth within the person. Do you count your addictions as bills? I'm just saying even a spoiled dog don't want a meatless bone. Do you want someone else's leftover rib tip after they've slobbered all over it? (There's a double loop ahead) Are you a personality worshiper? Do you know that God is a jealous God? Then explain to me how you could remain in a church were the pastor once preached against homo-sexuality, until God revealed and exposed the homo-sexual spirit which lied within the pastor, as he sat in the pulpit and exalted his wife and children all while living a lie? Do you now accept homo-sexuality only because it hit home through a father, mother, child or a love one? This is to all you women who act like men, all you men who act like women and to all of you who've had surgery to change your gender. You can't erase your memory or the memories of those who knew your gender from birth. Has homo-sexuality become your stumbling block? What or who shall separate you from the love of Christ? Did your family, children or friends become your stumbling block? Is Satan stealing your time with road blocks to derail you? Are you controlled by the spirit of lust as you head to the strip club bound by that nasty sex demon that you work overtime for? Wow. Instead of treating your wife and children you'd rather give your money to a sweaty stripper whom a many of hand as touched. While I'm at it here's something for you strippers; excuse me exotic dancers. You only get one body when you wear it out you can't get another one. Husbands have you ever stopped to think that after a night out in the strip club you go home climb in bed with your spouse and bring that spirit on her. This is for you married women that think you slick. Ladies night is for single woman your husband may think its innocent not knowing it's your excuse to get out and be naughty. (I'm not talking about you unless

I'm talking about you) He's none the wiser thinking he's married to a saved woman as he looks forward to your ladies night out because he can enjoy his standing appointment with his other lover. And you both call yourselves a Child of God as you break Gods commandment. (I did say it was a double loop) Are you guilty of pulling into the church parking lot smoking on your cigarette and blasting your worldly music as you park your car and run into the House of God and put on your choir robe? Are you deacon sip and tip? Are you mother curse? Are you elder ashtray? You tell me what's wrong with that line up because in some churches these are the very people who work the altar and have the audacity to try and pray someone through. When they have a cursing demon and their smelling like a ashtray with liquor on their breathe from the night before? (This is why you must be very careful when you allow someone to lay hands on you.) If this is you, God ain't in it you need a deliverance ministry. You need to be delivered and filled with the Holy Ghost because it's obvious you don't have Holy Ghost power. People of God listen up. God is looking for a holy people. So stop making excuses for your life, don't become addicted to reasoning, stop trying to figure out everything and let God do the God thing in your life. It's time for a new way of thinking; People of God it's time to stop making excuses and call a spade a spade. You must first except that these are spirits that lie within you and stop allowing Satan to bully you, take a stand and cut out the things that don't bare fruit in your life. God helps those that are willing to help themselves and know that if you live life long enough you will be wounded. The unsaved me could have held on to excuses and continued my path of hatred and bitterness toward men and life in general. She could have allowed Satan to have her cold-hearted and bound replaying the why's of her life. Why me? Over and over as she waxed old but instead she let go and let God. The unsaved me can think back to around the age of about seven years old when she first felt the spirit of fear. Someone living with her at the time said come here; she looked and knew something wasn't right and she ran away. She still remember the things that took place in the closet and the memories of certain ones who lusted behind her. These were men who should've protected her of all people she shouldn't have had to fear them but the foul spirits that lied within them caused them to have no shame, as they were quite bold with their aggressions, which caused her to have anxiety whenever she was around them. This became the terror of her life causing her to be labeled as the black sheep of the family. Whenever there was a gathering, she suffered the abuse of certain ones taunting her by rubbing against her inappropriately. You see it started at the age of ten and never stopped clear on up to her adult life. Am I telling your story that's buried deep within you? I'm talking about the dark secrets you drown in your debauchery. I know some of you by now are saying why you didn't tell someone. So to answer your thought "I did." It was said to me get over it you're not the only one it happens to its apart of being a girl. So I grew angry and said one day I'll be grown and I'm going to tell it. I've suffered grave abuse behind exposing the truth of my God awful life and not just from the unsaved but I've suffered an even greater abuse from the self-righteous. And even if I knew what I know now I would still tell my unsaved story I would just scream louder. You see I've found that people like gossip;

it's just so delicious to their ears. That's why it's so important that we as the Children of God take heed to the Word of God and eat the whole roll, that we may have the discipline to keep our minds on what so ever things are pure, what so ever things are honest, what so ever things are just, what so ever things are lovely, and what so ever things are of a good report. You see no one cared about my hurt but surely everyone wanted me to disclose the stars, businessmen, politicians and preachers. You see that would have been juicy in their mouth but she never intended to hurt anyone. She only intended to be free and she won't apologize for her testimony and in the same breathe she want allow Satan to use her to disclose another man's sin for capital gain. I must say To God be the glory. Not only did God heal her heart but God sent her a love and allowed her to love by renewing her in the spirit of her mind. You could say that those responsible for her failed to protect her but instead she choose to pray that one day they may be freed from their sins and filled with the Holy Ghost and she pray that they won't perish in their sins and that God would have mercy on them. And that goes to all of the self-righteous ones who persecuted her as well. You see she know that God will erase your past even when people dangle it in front of you. So we as christians must walk in a way to free others and remember to forgive is to forget. She was born in sin and shaped in iniquity. She came from a people who feed her beer from a baby on up, so she can honestly say she drank alcohol her entire unsaved life. Do you see when the spirit first entered her? Do you see who the spirit used and how they nourished the spirit within her throughout her childhood? It was nothing for her to drink a beer as a child and think nothing of it because that was normal life for her. At the age of fifth-teen she became pregnant so that meant she could drink openly and now entered the spirit of gambling. Her baby daddy wasn't a gambler so he would put the money on the table for her to gamble for him. I'm telling you everyone in the room was high off something, some on dope, coke, marijuana, pills, or liquor you name it and it was in the room. This was back in the day when people used blue light bulbs and you partied until you puked or passed out. The house would be smoked out with incense burning and blues playing as we'd party till the sun came up in a damp, dark, sweat filled musty room full of demonic spirits. Some crying, some fighting, some with their girlfriend not their wife and some with their wife and their girlfriend unbeknown to their wife. So here's when the spirit of adultery was exposed, you have to remember the spirit of lust entered at a very young age. This is the definition of being born in sin and shaped in iniquity out of an estrange people. Do you see how she was breaded up? Do you see how the spirits took root in her? These generational curses came through the blood line of her great-grandfather, great-grandmother, grandfather, grandmother, father and mother as they grew stronger and stronger within her. You see she can recall certain people who told her that this certain person was a hot mess, wearing her wigs with the hair so long she had to move it out the way just to sit down, long eye lashes, hot pants, drinking, smoking, cursing, gambling and controlling her man. Then came along another particular person with an even stronger spirit who was decked out, face painted, bound by the cursing spirit, adultery, and alcohol. She's unruly and reckless living a life of torment wrapped up, tied up and tangled up in the yoke of bondage. They say the unsaved me came along and magnified it times ten. It seemed as though every generational curse plus some fell upon her. But it was one thing I knew for sure and that was, I would protect those who I was responsible for and until this very day, I pray that their feet touch not my iniquity. Because of the severity of abuse I suffered I didn't take them around certain people or for that matter anywhere unless I was present. They was taught not to allow anyone to kiss them or not to sit on anyone's lap, not granddaddy, uncle, cousin I meant nobody. I would tell them if anyone touches you better tell me and remember I would say to them, if you don't tell me God will. As a result of her childhood and adult experiences, she might have almost just about smothered them. And in their very own words "the only thing we miss is the food" I'd just laugh and say "I'm glad because I couldn't afford to feed you now." You see she had no idea the life they lived until God saved her. They were rotten and her deliverance exposed it. You see they fought her tooth and nail because they didn't want to conform to her change of lifestyle. They were accustomed to vacationing, fine dining, designer clothing, skating, bowling, movies, amusement parks and the latest and greatest of everything. They never had to share anything and they didn't have to take turns watching television because each of them had their own big screen. Each of them had their own video game, they never knew what it was like to wear hand-me-downs or go to bed hungry and they never road in a jalopy. She served them like a slave as if they were kings and queen and even though she didn't spare the rod, she surely spoiled them all. But you see those were the days of old and once God got hold to her, her only words were, everyone that has breath in her house must serve God. And as a result they started dropping off like flies. Even the person in whom she patterned her life behind tried to suffocate her, as she recall how the person would call saying "you gone too far now, you done let that man brain wash you, you'll see, the church isn't what you think it is, you'll be back, and remember this one thing, blood is thicker than water, as the person would drive the nail into the coffin." As the unsaved me now recall, that person never ended a phone conversation without their signature line "you know where you been but you don't know where you're going." You wrong you wrong, how can you just up and leave us?" What about them? You not right, it just isn't right. She would respond by saying I'm just going on with God. My question still stands why is she so hated? This question is not limited to all of the self-righteous who tried to torment her and you know exactly who you are my darlings. Don't be mad with the saved me was always my respone I'm just obeying the Word of God. As she would say you no better there's nothing I can say to you concerning the Word of God because you know the truth and you've made your choice. As the saved me would end the phone conversation with you know I love you and I mean no disrespect or harm to you. There was a time in my life when I was void of the Word of God and now that I know better, I choose to do better. (As you read further you'll find that the saved me was hated by the self-righteous because of my testimony of the unsaved me) The Word of God tells us to come out from among them and be yea separate. So she obeyed. This was one of many trials for her as she traveled along her lonesome road. You see she was ridiculed, criticized, belittled, and ostracized.

All the saved me can say to you is the more she was attacked by religious spirits and the more the self-righteous abused and rejected the God in her, the thicker her skin became and the stronger she grew. Is your mouth a gate way thats full of cursing, bitterness and venomous poison? Are you like a vinegar jar, always got a sour face? Why are some of you still among people of darkness? I choose to keep Gods commandments and hold his statues. Is this your situation? You say you saved but you headed to the night club. So what it's your mother's fiftheth birthday party your mama needs deliverance. It's time to stop reaching back and ask yourself. How can I become an example to lead my family out of bondage, if I myself haven't gotten the victory? People of God don't get caught in the crevice of life and why would you take a gift from Satan at the cost of your soul? Stop buying lottery tickets, scratch cards, playing bingo and rolling dice, give up the casino, stop betting on your favorite sports team and horse because these things are not pleasing to God. Maybe this will help you; there won't be a slot machine in Heaven, there won't be a liquor store, smoke shop, strip club and you won't have your wife, your girlfriend and your partner to. I'm just saying if thats the case what do anyone need deliverance for and why did God send his Son Jesus? If you can answer that question have at it. How is it that you have the audacity to say God blessed you in the mist of your sin? I understand that God rain on the just and on the unjust but that doesn't mean that you won't pay the penalty for your sin. Now take a moment and ask yourself. Why do you give in to Satan? Oh, I guess I understand. If Satan's your father then you must obey him. So now my question has become don't you believe in the God you say you serve? Did you know that no man can serve two masters? You'll either love the one or hate the other. So stop indulging in the things that are not edifying to the body of Christ and began to live your life like the Child of God that you say you are. Replace these things with things which are becoming of a true Child of God. (Here comes a backwards loop remember you're on the roller coaster called the quiet storm) Its time to grow up and stop acting like a child you say you grown then be grown. You see some of you need to let go of your excuses for why you're still in your parents basement or sleeping in your childhood bedroom after thirty years. You say you grown, but you not grown, you just an over grown child who's afraid of the responsibilities of life. And some of you parents need to stop sucking the life out of your children by trying to live through them and after you dead and gone they become as lost puppies. It's time to get your priorities in order find you some Jesus and live Holy. The Word of God say's there is a way which seemeth right unto a man, but the end thereof are the ways of death. So why would you choose to live a sinful life to your demise. Are you living to live again? Are you burning the candle on both ends getting all you can get with no concern of judgment? Or does your lifestyle exemplify the gravitas of a true Child of God who's living to live again? (Spot check) Its ten o'clock, the kids are down, your wife is turning in for the night and you have an itch that your wife can't scratch. You are bound by the spirit of lust, as you kiss your wife and head toward the front door, as your wife turns over and pulls the cover over her head, while saying don't stay out to late, remember you have work tomorrow. Okay honey. As you reach for your phone to make contact with the other woman with only one thing in mind. And so it begins as she opens the door, and greets you with a kiss and a drink. You enter and therapy begins as you allow her spirit to massage into yours. (Look at that nasty stinking devil in action) She has the smell of oils with a hint of incense flowing throughout the house, as the sweet aroma of candles glimmer in the dark and the echo of music plays nice and mellow in the background. You see he's lead of his flesh and every time his flesh rares up he wants it satisfied. As he lives a lie bound by a sex addiction and fetishes. Are you the wife who doubles as a sex doll? Do you seek attention to cover your lack of self-esteem? Are you that married woman who still has a smorgasbord of men? Are you a woman who's always on the runway or should I say display? Styling in your five inch heels with your toes painted red like lollipops, bare legs, breast hanging out, long claw nails, horse hair and make-up to cover all your battle scars. And what's funny you're unaware that you look like a slab of meat for a dog. Yes. I'm talking about that pit-bull you laid up with that at any moment it can lock its jaws into your heart and rip it straight out your chest. If you don't understand that analogy listen to the stories of those who tried to commit suicide. Read about that man or woman who's on death row or doing life in prison they can surely tell you the destruction matters of the heart can cause. This is a Word to the Wise the two deadliest L's are love and lying both can land you in the lake of fire. I understand this sounds harsh but you see she can make a statement like that because she's been there when she was unsaved and the unsaved her sinned more than you can bear to read about but God! And to all you married women your wedding ring means nothing because your attire tells every man that you have no respect for your God, your husband or yourself. And when he slides up on you he proves it every time, you bitter want to be who say you're a Child of God but you need deliverance. When will you ladies stop allowing Satan to use you by giving way to seducing spirits? It's time to dress like a lady, cover up and stop prostituting yourself; don't you know sex sales and will send you to hell? Did you know that after you please your flesh it doesn't wash away with a shower but it becomes a soul tie? Just take a moment and think about everyone you pleasured and multiply it. Everytime you opened or entered someone you must count the one's they satisfied their flesh with. Are you one who married for stability or to cover up your homo-sexuality? Why are you avoiding the mirror? It's time to take a good look and examine yourself. People of God stop defining your life by someone else's life; don't you know it's not wise to live in comparison to another? Are you guilty of sizing yourself to the first lady of your church? Are you hiding behind these excuses? Well my first lady is sexy; her hair is blonde, she keep her nails and feet fire red, she even wear pants suits and blue jeans. I love her accessories, my first lady got mad swag. You so called sanctified folk need to get with it. Please, contrary to what some preachers preach this is a new day times have changed and yawl old school. All I have to say is you should be able to tell Gods people from worldly people and there's only one Holy Ghost. If you think I'm wrong, try to stop painting your finger nails and toes, whip off the make-up, stop cutting and dyeing your hair, take off those pants, lower your heels and buy clothes that fit. I know that this isn't a favorable teaching but try it and you'll see just how bound some of you really are. Truth be told some of you women want go to the mailbox let alone to the corner store or school house without make-up on. Take the earrings, bracelets, and gold chains off and watch the spirit rare up in you. If you don't believe me then try it, you'll see just how bound you really are. Watch and see how the spirit will begin to tell you that there's nothing wrong with a little bling bling or foundation. I'm not judging anyone; I'm just sharing the Word of God and my personal conviction. Think about it how often do you see a woman in baggy blue jeans? Ladies let's keep it real when you select a pair of blue jeans and try them on in most cases the first thing you do is squat down, kick both legs and pull the jeans all the way up at the thighs, all while sucking your stomach in. The next thing you do is turn around in the mirror to be sure that your tail bone is showing and then you check the split in the front. Now ladies be honest with yourself you do all of that in an attempt to cause men to lust behind you. That's why it's so important to read the Word of God, whereby you will know that the Bible gives us this intelligence (2 Timothy 3:6-7) For of this sort are they which creep into houses, and lead captive silly women laden with sins, led away with divers lusts, Ever learning, and never able to come to the full knowledge of the truth. You see the unsaved me been where you are and done that plus more. So ladies I'm not passing judgment on you I just thank God for the victory because truly I know that in times past the enemy used me as a tool which caused men to stumble and fall due to the spirit of lust. But through the hearing of the Word of God and out of my obedience to the Word of God I received my deliverance and the power of the Holy Ghost now keeps me, which means I'm no longer Satan's little helper. So ladies when you take those blues jeans off and put on dresses and skirts below your knees, you'll began to hear clothes talk for the first time. Trust me I know. So now I challenge those of you who think that you're strong enough to let go of your jeans and leggings. Grab a calendar make a check list tell your First Lady about the challenge and see how quick the spirit in her rises up for debate. I guarantee you that you're First Lady won't even entertain the conversation except to point out a particular denomination to justify her belief. Which poses my next question. Have you chosen a denomination because it fits your lifestyle? (Deuteronomy 22:5) Woman shall not wear that which pertaineth unto a man, neither shall a man put on a woman's garment for all that do so are a abomination unto the Lord thy God. (1 Timothy 2:9-10) In like manner also, that women adorn themselves in modest apparel, with shamefacedness and sobriety; not with braided hair, or gold, or pearls, or costly array. But (which becometh women professing godliness) with good works. All I can say to you is the Bible is for the believer! Now you tell me. Can a man go to an all-male store and pick out a dress, panties with a booty inside, heels with a matching handbag and a pair of panty hose? Or does the cross dresser have to go to a woman's store? Ladies this is for you. Just because pants are in the women's department doesn't justify them as woman's apparel. This is a Word to the Wise align yourself with the Word of God and be not deceived. Question. Has fashion become your stumbling block? People of God time is winding up so stop living by the mouth of others read the Word of God for yourself and find an anointed Man of God and Woman of God with a track record exemplifying holiness. Stop flocking to these churches were the pastor is telling stories to those of you with itching ears. As he feeds you promises of blessings through motivational speaking, psychology and lectures that were put together by his paid research staff and not from the revelation of God. Now how can you argue with the truth? If you don't believe me than ask him if you can get close enough to him. A fly would get more attention than you ever will. So now my question is. Could you reach him when you needed strength not to light up that cigarette, drink that shot or do that blow? Maybe you needed someone to calm you before you beat your wife or swallowed that bottle of pills. Unless you belong to a church that never preaches sin only prosperity, so you think those things are pleasing and acceptable to God. And all the while you die a slow but show death as you run around from church to church trying to buy a miracle when all you need is the Holy Ghost down on the inside. This is a Word to the Wise the gift of salvation is free and the price has already been paid for us all. Don't you know that Jesus was the ultimate sacrifice and all you have to do is give him a life? (Brace yourself) Has the spirit of division become your stumbling block causing you to separate from your God? I'm reminded of how someone planted seeds of discord. As I recall them telling others that they were now grown and that they could now make their own decisions and that they no longer needed my approval. So the cockatrice seeds were planted within them as they would tell them that's her life you got your own life to live. They broke them down by saying to them yawl don't have to stay there in that boring life you can come with me. She pushing her saved life you need to live and find God for yourselves and just as the enemy intended the seeds took root and began to burst one by one. And as a result they all became disobedient and defiant against the rules of the house, packed their bags, laughed in her face and moved out into the world. She still have a visual of the stanky leg down the front stairs; as she stood crying in the window in disbelief. Every day I pray God will have mercy on them and every day I bind all foul and contrary spirits and plead the blood of Jesus over them. I can honestly say it's been one thing after another. Talk about a raging storm my God, all I can say is never, never, never give up. If there is one fact concerning the saved me If she's done with you: she's done with you. If she gives you her word it is as good as gold and if she speaks a word to you or tells you a dream concerning you whether it be good or bad it's sure to come to pass. I'm telling you this God she found had everybody stirred up! She's reminded of one day while at work someone stopped her in passing and said to the saved her. I don't know how you do it, I couldn't live without a drink and whatever God it is you came in contact with I don't want him you can keep that God all to yourself honey. She replied. "It's not me it's the Holy Ghost that keeps me and it will keep you if you want to be kept." And by the way young lady did you know they'll be no liquor in heaven? Have a wonderful day as she continued on her way. What she found so puzzling was how the so called saved folks would tell the saved her that they were so glad that God saved her like he saved them and how they could see the God in her life. Hear me now. These were the same people whom she once drank in the parking lot with or maybe even partied with, or possibly traveled with, who were still in bondage, yet they believe that they are saved. Is it something wrong with this picture or is it just me? I can't even count the number of times that I heard girl what's wrong with you? You done got all religious and gone crazy in God. I think of how quick they would say I'm a Child of God, I'm blessed, I'm just not as religious as you are. And what scares me is they really believe that lie. Talk about strong delusion. Let me drop this little nugget. Your car, house, clothes and money don't make you blessed. Did you know that Satan gives gifts too? So every time you lay on your back, dance for a bill, movie, pair of gym shoes, or to get your rent and car note paid, you might as well accept the fact that you've taking a gift from your provider which is the enemy. And every time you pay a bill, give a dollar bill; get her hair, nails and feet done and she's not your wife, Satan has used you as his supplier. Did you know that lying and cheating is not of God, stealing and abortion is not of God, anxiety, anger, and hatred is not of God, jealousy, love of money and envy is not of God? This is just a self-examination. There won't be a crap game in heaven or slot machine, no night club or strip club and you won't have worldly music. You must first learn to praise and worship God, keep God's commandments, holds God's statues, live free from sin and be obedient on this side. You tell me. If you can't let go your cigarette, liquor, extra affairs, gambling, sexual addictions on this side. What makes you think that you can take those things into heaven? People of God you must be rooted and grounded without wavering, standing by faith, leaning and trusting in the Lord until the day Jesus returns. Remember a double minded man is unstable in all his ways. Which raises the question. How can the so called born again christian go to church, hear the Word of God yet refuse to receive sound instruction? How can you leave the House of God and head straight to the liquor store? What about those of you who are using foul language before you exit the front doors of the church house? Let's not forget to mention those of you who are lighting your cigarette and turning on you worldly music before you even make it out the parking lot as you head to the watering hole or to pull that one arm bandit with your offering. Yes that offering the offering that you allowed that demonic spirit to talked you out of given. (I'm not trying to hurt you I'm trying to help you) Ask yourself do you truly have the Holy Ghost? How can you leave the House of God after hearing the Word of God and do everything against Gods perfect will for your life? Do you have a religious spirit? Do you have the spirit of debate which is a trap that so many denominational christians fall into? Are you guilty of vowing to God and failing to keep your vow? How many times have you cried out begging God to rectify a situation in your life? Whether it was curing cancer, blessing you when you were bearing, keeping you from becoming homeless or maybe it was sparing your life. So you cry out Lord if you just help me this time, I promise I won't do it again; I'll give my life over to serving you God. God please! Please God! I beg of You! The situation has you so broken that the snot from your nose is running into your mouth as you kneel or in some cases people have fallen prostrate at the foot of the hospital bed of their spouse, parent, child or maybe even for yourself and God inclines his ear unto you and accepts the prayer from your lips as God blesses you miraculously. If you were ever in that situation and you cried out to God for a miracle. I want to know when God answered your prayer, did you keep your promise to God?It's amazing how quickly some people forget their promises and their vow to God once the trial has passed. (Ecclesiastes 5:4-5) When thou vowest a vow unto God, defer not to pay it; for he hath no pleasure in fools: pay that which thou hast vowed. Better is it that thou shouldest not vow, than that thou shouldest vow and not pay. This is a Word to the Wise you may be able to shuck and jive people; but you'll never be able to shuck and jive God. Do you have a story of someone who had fallen gravely ill to the degree of life support. Certain people were stirred up and one of them was an emotional wreck. You see she and the saved her know longer had a relationship. The only time they spoke was when she called to tell the saved her she was wrong for chosen a man and his God over them. Her saved life brought forth hatred, evil intent and animosity towards her from lets just say everybody the saved and the unsaved. As they passed judgment on the saved her concerning her deliverance and sewed seeds of discord within others. So all the saved her could do was say a prayer over the phone with. Twenty-four hours had now passed and the phone rang "their condition has worsened their not breathing on their own and the doctors are preparing for the worse." If you want to see them alive you need to come to the hospital because it's not looking good. She replied "It Is well God told me it is well." The saved her then asked her if she remembered the dream she told her about? She replied. "Yes I remember." You see about three months prior the saved her had a dream. She wrote the dream down and the next day she called her and asked her if she could tell her about a dream she had? The person on the other end of the phone took a deep breathe, paused and then said "ok." The saved her begin to tell her that it wasn't such a nice dream and that in the dream that particular person was in a hospital bed. There were tubes connected to them everywhere and in the dream she went to the hospital to pray at their bed-side it was night time. After she prayed the Lord spoke. "It is well." It was now the third day of them being in the hospital she was at work and her phone began to ring back to back it was about 5pm and she was unable to answer the phone at the time of the calls. After she completed her shift as she headed to her car the phone rang again it was her. Hello "please you must come to the hospital please." As her words echoed in her ear. At first the saved her was reluctant to go because she had also had a dream that she would be attacked when she arrived at the hospital. But she replied. "Ok I'll come to the hospital for you; for you I will come. The saved her preceded home prepared her husband's dinner served him and changed her clothes, as her husband anointed her with oil while praying for her. Remember your dream he said; as she responded yes preacher. As he was making reference to a previous dream she had concerning her being attacked. She grabbed her hat, coat, purse and proceeded to the hospital. When she arrived she took a moment and prayed for herself before she exited her car and she continued to pray until she entered the hospital. She stopped at the front desk and was directed to the intensive care unit, as she walked toward their room she was greeted by the person who requested that she come. A certain person jumped up in rage another person stepped up to shake her hand, as she reached out to embrace the person who requested that she come. My exact words were "I need to go in their room alone." The person was in intensive care so the only people that could hear or see her were the doctors and nurses. She began to call on the name of Jesus, as she walked from side to side back and forth along side their hospital bed, clapping her hands pleading the Blood of Jesus, calling forth healing and total restoration as she binded the spirit of death and spoke life in Jesus name. As she continued to pray saying by faith I decree and declare in the name of Jesus that they will fully recovery for Father in Heaven you showed me this and you told me that "it is well" and I say to you that it is so. Upon leaving the room she spoke the words it is well, I say it is well in the Lord Hallelujah. The staff was quiet and at attention. As she put on her hat, coat and grabbed her purse nodded her head toward the doctor and walked out to the waiting room were everyone had gathered. She reached out toward the person who asked her to come to the hospital and as she extended her hand toward her and they made contact she began to say. The God I serve is a super-natural God. He's a miracle working God. I touch and agree with you right now in the name of Jesus that they will fully recover. Their organs will be completely restored, their mind will be intact, they will have the activities of their limbs and in the name of Jesus they will leave this hospital Alive!" For it is well I said to her. Hear me when I say to you it is well. Through her trembling and tears she looked up at the saved her and said "I don't have it, I don't have faith like you do." Don't you see them? They not breathing on their own and right now we're making preparations. Look at me as the saved her called her by her name and stated "there has not been any dream or vision good or bad, that God has shown me that haven't come to pass" you have to believe it is well she said to her. As she cried out in response not everyone has the same faith, as tears ran down her face uncontrollably. She began to tell the saved her that she needed help and that she needed to do better and that she didn't have it, as she looked eye to eye at the saved her. Suddenly! Out of nowhere came screams and profanity. Your day will come to see your mother on her death bed and I can't wait. I will be the first one to come and laugh in your face. These were the very words that came out of their mouth with hatred and murder in their eyes toward the saved her. Now remember they're talking about their very own love one. Now there's a deep voice saying with aggression what is she doing here? She don't have any business at the hospital. Now someone else is hollering. Didn't I tell you not to say anything to that girl? As they grab their phone and begin to call others. Remember we're inside the hospital and this person is yelling at the top of their voice. Hurry up she at the hospital yawl need to get here right away. The person who went bye me earlier in rage; who is also the person who said they couldn't wait until the other person died so they could laugh in my face has now launched toward me. Remember you're on the quiet storm and you're in the middle of a winding turn so the story is twisting and turning as you read it because it just may be that you may have experienced this same event in your very on life. The saved her stood up and spoke directly to the demonic spirit that was operating thru the attacker, as she began to cast all manner of evil to the pit of hell and plead the blood of Jesus against it. Now that deep voice is saying "Stop, please stop, don't pray that again." The one that was on the phone calling everyone to the hospital to attack her is now saying "okay it's like that?" Alright were the words that the attacker uttered as the saved her continued to pray

47

and cast the demonic spirit to the dry places where it belonged. That's enough please stop praying the attacker said as they grabbed her and began dragging her down the halls of the hospital. The person who called the saved her to the hospital is crying with their hands on their head saying "leave this is my family just leave." Well my question is what was I? By now security has arrived as the staff was in disbelief. What's going on? As the nurses came toward the saved her saying "we're so sorry this has happened to you, after all we just witnessed you do at that persons bedside. The saved her lifted her hands toward the Lord and said I came in peace to believe God for a miracle. You called me to the hospital and I told you that I wouldn't be welcome amongst those people. Have a wonderful night as she folded her hands and walked to her car binding all foul and contrary demonic spirits along the way. About ten hours later her phone rings. Did they call you yet? No she replied. Man after you left the hospital that person is no longer on life support, their eyes are open and they even talking. Man I know they glad you came; you scared all of them. I replied it's not me, it was all God. I'll talk to you later thanks for the update. Shortly after she calls. "Thank you, thank you." I said to God be the glory for he is faithful that promised. How quickly we forget Gods miracles. If you're confused after reading that scenario I'm just as confused after writing it but what I will say. That was a great example of what the possibility of death will bring out of a persons emotions. Instead of believing God on one accord the lack of faith of others, shows it's evil face. When will you come out of bondage, get yourself delivered and stop lying to God? For there's hell to pay? Can you believe after God performed that miracle the saved her was told. "You need to be sure that the God you pray to is the right God." Not only does this person have a spirit of debate concerning denominations but look at the cockatrice egg Satan used them to plant within the saved her in hopes that it would one day burst. I can't count the number of times I've heard it doesn't take all that sense I've been saved. People actually tell me that my life is just too extreme and that it don't take all that. Girl that way of living was back in the days of old, child we living in a different time. The Devil is a liar! If you pick up your Bible and read it you will find out that the very same things happening now were happening then. Man wants to reword the Bible to fit his own understanding or justify his sins. This hasn't blind-sided God. God is so far ahead of man he told man in the Bible don't add to his Word and don't take away from his Word. If that doesn't prove to you that God is eons ahead of man nothing will. (You are now upside down on the roller coaster) Homo-sexuality didn't just hit the scene. So it don't matter how your pastor choice to avoid preaching on the spirit of homo-sexuality. If the people of times past didn't get away with it then, you surely won't get away with it now. People of God you need to read inspirational books of truth pertaining to the miracles God have performed in ordinary people such as yourselves, that it may help to build your faith. You so called believers need to put down worldly demonic books and get in your bible that you may become more knowledgeable concerning the truth; as it relates to the Word of God. Why do you poison your mind with things that aren't edifying to the body of Christ? How can you say you love God but you spend no time with God? Some of you have no prayer life and won't fast even though the Word of God say's that something's only come out by fasting and praying, yet you such the christian. I'm not talking to the reprobate. Meaning you unprincipled people, rogue, scoundrel and good-for-nothing degenerate a sinner who is predestined to damnation. She didn't call you any of those things; she just gave you the definition. She not talking to those of you who have been given over to strong delusion, misconception, misapprehension, error or misbelief and resistant to reason. She not talking to those of you that have a false belief or opinion strongly held, as if having a mental disorder. To sum it all up. She not talking to those of you who've been rejected by God and beyond hope. This is a Word to the Wise for those of you who didn't know. There is a such thing as a vessel unto honor, and a vessel unto dishonor. That's why it's important to know your craft as a true Child of God. Tell me how can you be a Child of God without a sword? The Word of God says (Romans 12:1-2) I beseech you therefore, brethren, by the mercies of God, that ye present your bodies a living sacrifice, holy, acceptable unto God, which is your reasonable service. And be not conformed to this world: but be ye transformed by the renewing of your mind, that ye may prove what is good, and acceptable, and perfect, will of God. Don't you want to have your own personal experience with God? For as sure as her name is Rahab God is real, God is alive, God is a healer, delivery, the Lord of a break through, God is a mind regulator, God is hope, peace, love, a need meeter, a way maker, a strong tower, a rock in a weary land, a miracle working God. He is the great I Am, that I Am, I Am. God is all that and more Hallelujah, Hallelujah, Hallelujah. She's so very grateful

God didn't give her over to reprobation despite her enormous iniquity, rebelliousness and disobedience. God yet saved and delivered her from out of a horrible pit and despair. She was in times pass uncontrollable, full of anger, always looking for confrontation and blaming everyone else but herself. She was what you would call a radical sinner. She didn't care whether she lived or died. Yet what amazes her the most is that she was unaware that she was already dead while living in sin. Through her deliverance she learned that in order to live she had to die to the world and become born again, that she may be in the world but not of the world. She's so glad she's been washed by the blood of the lamb and filled with the Holy Ghost that through Jesus Christ she's no longer a slave to sin. She will forever give unto the Lord the glory due unto his name; She will worship the Lord in the beauty of holiness all the days of her life and every day that the Lord gives her breathe in her body. She will testify and speak of his super-natural ability to heal, deliver and set free. You see she know what it means to say thank you Jesus for keeping her clothe and in her right mind because there was a time in her life that the enemy attacked her mind to the point of hearing voices. So she can truly thank God for mind regulation. She understand what it means to say thank you Jesus for the activity of her limbs because during the birth of her first child her nerves were crushed which caused her to be paralyzed on her left side for a short time. So she unequivocally knows what it means to thank God for total healing and restoration. You see she's not just a pretty face with long flowing hair; she's full of substance. (St John 10:9-10, 28) I am the door: by me if any man enter in, he shall be saved. I am come that they might have life, and that they might have it more abundantly. I give unto them eternal life; and they shall never perish, neither shall any man pluck them out of my hand. People of God this is a Word to the Wise it's imperative that you abide in the Word of God. Don't just say you holy live holy for holy, holy, holy it's a lifestyle. Eat this spiritual vitamin along the way. Don't be classified as a whore or whoremonger but be yeah holy a peculiar people a royal priesthood. Ladies no more entering the House of God bare legged but wear stockings which becomes that of a lady. Buy skirts and dresses with enough material so you won't have to pull them down when you stand up or tug on them while you're sitting. Ladies hide your knee caps, cover your collar bone and loosen up your attire so that every time you stand to praise God you won't have to nip and tuck. Remember tight clothes show not only you're shape but your muffin top to. I know it might read harshly but you look like you got a booty in the front and in the back. Not to mention people can count your dimples and ladies trust me when I say it's not jealousy, it just don't look good. To everyone else you look like a pig in a blanket or an egg waiting to crack. This is a Word to the Wise if it's tight when you try it on it's even tighter with a girdle. So for God sake stop thinking that once you put your foundation on the clothes will fit foundation only helps the jiggle. And every woman who wears a girdle can't wait to take it off especially after she eat. Men I have just one question for you. Sense when did men start showing their shape? Jeans so tight look like it hurt and suits a size to small. Who are you dressing to impress women or men? My brother if this is you; the women are left with a question mark? Do you realize that designers have lured you in with the phrase metro-sexual? What is unisex cologne or perfume? People are down for anything and everything ain't no shame and ain't know limits and they dare you to oppose them. Some people are ostracized because they believe differently. Where do you draw the line at one's right to believe or should I say your right to believe? Who gave man the authority to tell the People of God what they must accept in opposition concerning the Word of God? Who gave man the authority to change God's divine order of nature? Sense when does a man get his eye-brows trimmed and shaped? I'm talking about a man; I hear you saying ain't nothing wrong with that. These are just thought provoking questions. Do you remember the commercial when out of nowhere there appeared half a tail bone hanging out swaying back and forth with a yellow thong showing, dazzy dukes and a halter top bending down over a juke-box and after selecting a song the person turned around and it was a man? How many men do you think felt violated after such a perverted commercial? Now a day anything and everything goes you can't watch television without two men or two women making out as if thats normal. I'll tell you what it is. It's Satan at work because the more perversion he can put before you the more you'll feel comfortable with it but it will never be the norm. People of God this is a Word to the Wise never forget to guard your gate. Have you seen some of these programs of so called christian people acting worse than the world? What kind of an example are you setting for those who truly won't to know Jesus when they watch your program and see you acting ugly? I could only imagine some people saying if her husband is a pastor and they do this or their kids do that and they say that they are a Child of God. Then I must be a Child of God too because I'm doing the very same things that the Man of God and Woman of God are doing. People of God you should be able to recognize a false prophet whenever you see or hear one. A Man of God and Woman of God life should be an example of holiness. Tell me why are you so easily deceived and persuaded? Haven't you read your Bible? Don't you know God is coming back for a holy people, holy meaning pure, incorruptible and blameless without spot or blemish. Did you know the enemy comes to fight your faith? Did you know that your mind is the battle ground? The enemy will tell you that everyone sins and once you give way to a thought that wasn't even yours. The fight of the advisory in your life has won by destroying your faith in God. People of God yes we were all born in sin and shaped in iniquity but through Jesus you no longer have to be subject to sin. That's why it's important that you be rooted and grounded in God. So instead of you receiving a thought of the enemy shout back by saying Satan, God has promised me! I am more than a conquer, I have the power to tread over serpents and greater is he who is in me. People of God you must activate the Word of God and apply it to every situation in your life on a daily bases. God has given you the power to bind so why aren't you using your power? Bind that homo-sexual spirit that lingers around your home and your child. Bind the spirit of poverty that's in your life, bind that nasty stinking demonic spirit of lust that's after your spouse, bind the spirit of slothfulness, bind the spirit of unforgiveness, bind that rebellious spirit, lying spirit, cursing spirit, back biting spirit, tale baring spirit and gossiping spirit. While you're at it bind the spirit of alcoholism, spirit of gambling I bind you in the name of

Jesus, spirit of suicide and murder I bind you in the name of Jesus, confused spirit, spirit of unbelief doubt and weariness I bind you in the name of Jesus. People of God it's through Holy Ghost Power that you are able to bind these demonic spirits up and sling the blood of Jesus on everything that's not like God in your life and in your home. People of God why aren't you using your God given power? Why are you allowing the enemy to wear you out and steal from you? You have the power why don't you use it? If God has promised you something I don't care if it's been thirty years and you still waiting hold on and continue to wait on God. Because it's a shame to say that some of you will take off work and lose pay just to wait on the cable man all day. Then you'll pray that he shows up yet you'll give up on God. People now a day want a suddenly and if they don't get it by the time frame they put on it they get mad and turn away from God. Is this you? Have you turned away from God? Has a divorce, a death, a diagnosis, a religious conversion caused you to turn away from God? People of God I don't care how long it takes wait on God for he is faithful that promised and while you're waiting, tell God I don't mind waiting on you Lord. This is a Word to the Wise hold on to the promises of God and while you're holding on do all things without murmuring and complaining. She remembers when she was yet working for transit and God spoke to her while driving up a hill as the sun was rising. "It won't be forever yet a little while." She knew instantly that greater was to come in her life and that one day would suddenly become her last day of employment with transit. She didn't know when, she didn't know how but by faith she believed the words that God had spoken to her. You see being married to a Man of God she needed sunday's off, not to mention she needed to be off work by a certain time daily. But transit is based solely on seniority and even though she had fourteen years of full-time service it didn't guarantee that she could pick sunday as her off-day. It seemed like every pick got worse and worse for her. She could hear the voice of the Man of God saying "you got to get it sweet heart you got to go through without complaining." Sweet heart you'll grow when you learn to praise your way through every situation, circumstance and trial. Then and only then will God move for you my love. You must remember the Word of God says do all things without murmuring and complaining. The Man of God meant business and he always laid the gauntlet down. I'm telling you sure enough as she applied the teaching of the Word of God; the dam broke loose in her life and for her life all to the glory of God. For as sure as she's writing and you're reading God has aligned her in his perfect will for her life. You see she let go and let God have his way. For there is one thing she surely learned, it got to be God and you got to be ready. To the hearer he is faithful that promised. She's no longer with transit and by faith she received because she believed and she didn't allow seventy plus thousand a year to cause her to miss the greater reward. So many people have prolonged the call on their life due to fear of change or should I say the unknown. We as the Children of God must remember his ways are not our ways and his thoughts are not our thoughts. God's ways are past our understanding and remember without faith it's impossible to please God. It's time to get out of the shallow water and go into the deep. How do you expect higher heights and deeper depths yet you sitting like a bump on a log watching the waves in the water while you disbelieve your own day dream. Faith is an action word and faith without works is dead! I can say by faith Rahab. Can you say by faith_____? People of God stop allowing yourselves to become hypnotized by false prophets of the world who water down the Word of God for capital gain. And while we're at it, what about those prosperity preachers and prophets who charge you to prophecy? They got you running from church to church and town to town paying for a prophetic word and in some cases they're prophesying a lie, while your soul is on the way to hell. Oh and by the way what's the difference in paying for a prophecy, going to a fortune teller, tarot card reader, psychic or palm reader? Hear me loud and clear I speak not against Prophets or Prophecy for I myself have accepted my gift as a Prophet. But ask yourself why pay my way to hell when I can go for free? Let me help somebody. Be yea holy for I am Holy, you got to live holy and remember holy holy holy it's a lifestyle. Do you know that God is a God of order? So explain to me how some of you can get a personal trainer and follow every rule that they give you to achieve your personal weight goal to the point of starvation and dehydration? But when the Preacher say's stop smoking, drinking, cursing, fornicating, gossiping, gambling, shacking, lying, cheating and stealing which free's your soul from the bondage of sin, he just became the devil. As you sit in church with rocks in your jaws and turn your nose up. This is for all you leaders. Don't you know that God has his choices and it's surely not a jelly back, spineless Man of God or Woman of God who sits on their throne in the church bound by the enemy and scared to preach the gospel? Abortion is murder! Homo-sexuals, lesbians, bi-sexuals, transgenders, queers and transsexuals are a abomination! You can try to exclude all these things you just read from the Bible and replace it with inclusion or say all God want us to do is love one another. But it will never be so because if God allows you to get away with it he'll have to raise all the dead he slew in Sodom and Gomorrah. Why you mad at me? I didn't make the rules, I just follow them and by the way God didn't ask for our opinion or approval anyway. How many times have you instructed your children not to play with fire or maybe you told them to stop fighting their sisters and brothers or maybe you said to them if you go in my purse without asking that's stealing? Was it don't do the nasty? It could've been the importance of getting an education? Maybe it was don't hang out with trouble makers, don't drink or smoke and above all don't lie to me? Or are you the parent that despised your strict upbringing, yes sir, no ma'am, may I, please, thank you, and excuse me? How many of you lived by these rules? When the street lights came on you knew to be in the house, you took naps, girlfriend or boyfriend was unacceptable, you cleaned your own bedrooms and back talk accompanied a back hand? Has that same hard headed child grown up and become you? You wouldn't obey your parents as a child and as an adult you won't obey God. Are you still living in the past and blaming everybody else for your heartaches and mistakes? Are you a person who has an excuse for everything? Let me give you an example. Some of you ladies are hiding behind this excuse. I don't have a husband because of something that happened to me ten years ago. Ladies it's time to stop treating every man you meet like the one who beat you, misused you, left you or cheated on you. Can I say this? You don't have a husband because you go out in the street with a rag on your head, dressed in the pajamas that you slept in the night before looking just how you smell, stinky. This is a Word to the Wise it's time to clean up your act. You've tried everything else in life so why not try Jesus? I'm talking about trying Jesus for real! It's time out for playing in the Church House why not go all in for the Lord? Just like you did for that man or woman who caused you to be bankrupt. I'm talking about that man or woman that you loved above your God. Yep! That's the relationship I'm reminding you of, that love that you never felt in your life until you meet that spirit. Yes I'm talking about that man or woman who broke your heart you couldn't eat or sleep and you thought because you swallowed a bottle of pills he or she would come back. And some of you men are guilty of stalking, calling leaving twenty messages, hiding in the garbage can and switching cars with your friend so you can watch her house. She's speaking from experience and she's not done. Some of you women have given your children away for a man or believed a man over your child when your child told you that he was touching them. You were so in love with the passion and emotion of that demonic spirit, that you ignored the cries of your very own child. You'll never be able to convince Rahab that demonic spirits aren't real. This is a Word to the Wise the love you're looking for is not in the world, it's not in a man or woman and it's not in material things. The love that you're looking for is in Christ Jesus. Jesus is the only one who can fill the void in your heart, Jesus is the only one who can heal you, deliver you and set you free. Not a man, not a woman, not your money, not your dog, cat, mother, father, sister, brother, cousin, that pill, that sex, that drink, that smoke or that demonic spirit that you lend your ear to. Oh and while I'm at it, for the love of Jesus stop waiting on that man in jail who walked you like a dog. Why would you marry a jail bird? What's wrong with you? Don't be boo boo the fool or stuck on stupid? She's not trying to hurt you she's trying to help you because she's been there and done that. It amazes me how one could love someone more than they love themselves. You got him looking like the board of health while you look like a rag doll. Why dress him for the other woman? It's time to put your feelings in your pocket, give your heart to Jesus and wait until your break through comes. The saved her is just trying to say to you why would you settle for less, when you can live Gods perfect will for your life? All you have to do is surrender and turn from your wicked ways. She turned from her wicked ways and all she can say is what the Word of God say's. O taste and see that the Lord is good: for blessed is the man that trusteth in him. God can do anything but fail, try him, you'll see. God healed her broken heart and took all her pains and fears away. People of God cherish your love affair with God and stop cheating on God and remember God is a jealous God. Just like you don't won't to be someone's second God won't be second. If God is not your first love God will allow you to be consumed by your first love all the way to a burning hell. I'm just saying, it's as simple and cut dry as that but its your choice to make. The saved her is giving you a friendly reminder that all souls belong to God but the soul that sinneth it shall surely die. You're free to do what you will but upon your death comes your judgment. It doesn't matter whether it's your father, mother, sister, brother, cousin, child, co-worker, aunt, uncle or dog. The Word of God says what fellowship does righteousness have with unrighteousness and what commune does light have with darkness. Anything you yield your spirit to that's not of God or becoming that of a Child of God has overtaking you. You may ask the question how is that? Because you no longer yield to the spirit of God, yet you choose to satisfy your flesh and be led by Satan. You tell me why do you love the world more than you love God? Is this your favorite line? When God is ready for me he'll change me. Don't you know that God is of a free will? That's why it's so important that you understand (Colossians 1:16) For by him were all things created, that are in heaven, and that are in earth, visible and invisible, whether they be thrones, or dominions, or principalities, or powers: all things were created by him, and for him: And he is before all things, and by him all things consist. So why would you choose to follow anything less than God? Except you love the world and are bound by the things thereof. Such as club hopping, gambling, drinking, smoking, fornicating, shacking up, strip clubs, and worldly churches who preach inclusion? (yes worldy churches) The Word of God tells us (1 John 2:15-16) Love not the world, neither the thing that are in world. If any man love the world, the love of the Father is not in him. For all that is in the world, the lust of the flesh, and the lust of the eyes, and the pride of life, is not of the Father, but is of the world. People of God it's time to stop mixing the pot of your mind with what other folks say let God be true and every man a liar with the understanding that this is an individual walk. "Old folk say too many cooks spoil the soup." So it's time to stop allowing Satan to trick you by causing you to become double-minded.

Choose this day whom ye will serve for no man can serve two masters he'll either love the one and hate the other or hold to the one and despise the other for no man can serve God and mammon. Did you know that many people have died and ended up in hell as a result of a sick perverted and twisted mind set? I'm going to give my life to Christ when I'm fifty or sixty years old but right now I'm young so I'm going to live it up. Are you one who makes that statement? Do you really believe that you can tell God at what age you'll choose to serve him? Seriously though for real, for real, I'm seriously asking you this question if you're the one who's making that statement? Did you know that your next breathe isn't promised to you? No man knows the day nor the hour. But there's one thing that we all know for sure and I'm scared of you if you're not scared of this fact: you will not escape death and then comes judgment. Through her deliverance she learned that though she thought she was alive, she was really dead and thru the death of the unsaved her, she now lives. You see some people only have the experience of death through a funeral but she lived her funeral up close and personal while she was yet still alive. You see everything she loved she had to let go. She's been inside her coffin and yet she stood on the outside of her coffin all at the same time. So she would like to share with you what she learned through her deliverance from darkness into the marvelous light. People of God her life is a true testament that the will of God want lead you to a place where God's grace can't keep you. She died to the world and was born again and thats when the people of the world began to treat the saved her like a stranger. They didn't want anything to do with the saved her except to hinder the God in her life by throwing her unsaved life into her saved life. You see someone very close to her in whom she looked up to became one of her greatest battles. She can recall the many times that person would call her and how unpleasant the tone of that persons voice was as that person always tried to break the saved her down and tell the saved her how wrong she was for choosing God over her. Because as quiet as it's kept that's all it was about everyone only cared about her leaving them and not the fact that she had gained salvation. She had found that white porch and she didn't care who walked by and threw stones, nothing was going to cause her to come off that white porch and lose her salvation. She finally had peace in her life and she found comfort in knowing that she had given those she was responsible for the best life possible and no demon in hell was going to cause her to believe anything less. Those phone calls never stopped. Ring, ring, ring. Hello. "You'll find out about the so called church folk they'll treat you worse than the people of the world, just you wait and see." All she could do was cry and hold the phone because she had to respect the person who was on the other end. "You'll never be excepted in the church; they'll never except a woman like you watch you'll see." She would just cry, cry, cry and hold the phone until they were done and after she hung up the phone she would cry some more. She was truly broken but she'd found Jesus and she wasn't letting go. When she said "no demon in hell was going to turn her away from her Lord and Savior Jesus Christ." She truly meant NO DEMON not even you. Yes, you with your ungodly opinion towards a Word to the Wise. "You've gone to far the church world isn't what you think it is remember I've been there and you don't know where you're going but you know where you been." The calls always ended with you wrong, you wrong. "This isn't God, this isn't God. Blood is thicker then water, you'll be back just you wait and see you'll be back." You've been brain washed was always the last words as they hung up the phone. Every time my phone rang it was some kind of demonic attack from the person on the other end. Ring, ring, ring. Hello. "You'll get bored soon and you'll be right back to your old ways." Ring, ring, ring. Hello. Just because you changed your life and married a Man of God don't mean you can't still hang out with us. Even though we drink and smoke we are still Children of God plus you were worse then all of us put together. Ring, ring, ring. Hello. "I just called to tell you that you been brain washed." Good morning she stated as she checked in with the window clerk at work. The person standing behind her say's to her girl whatever God you got, I don't want no part of as they would high five the person standing beside them while waiting to check in with the window clerk. Wow! Look at the reformed nun as the crowd would mock her. How do you do it? Tell me how because I can't live without a drink, a smoke and multiple partners. Here comes the mysterious voice. She just taking religion to serious, it don't take all that, she done gone from wild to crazy. Can you imagine what it feels like to hear someone say to you "I hate this new person you've become?" People were purposely cruel and rude toward her and she was even physically pushed while at work on several occasions. The attacks had got so bad that one morning a unknown person spoke out against the people who were openly aggressive towards the saved her. These were people that wouldn't so much as look her in her face when she was unsaved because the unsaved her had people fearful of her. She's revealing these things to show you how Satan was using people through demonic influences. She was attacked on every end as satan used those she knew to try and break her down. "You not fun anymore, I don't know you anymore, I want the old you back, sense you married that pastor you act old, I wish you would've never meet that preacher." Then there were those who would say "He is controlling you, he know you pretty thats why he make you dress like a old lady because he know you have a nice shape so he wants to cover your hips and thighs." That preacher man got you looking frumpy which was someone's favorite description of the saved me. Out of everything that was stated to me it never failed that every woman would say "You got your own mind remember he's just a man don't tell him everything something's you need to keep to yourself." I'm telling you she was poisoned and attacked on every end possible, not just physically but mentally, and spiritually. But she was holding up her shield quenching all the fiery darts of the wicked. She truly believed the Word of God and she activated it daily via any and every situation or circumstance. She was going to walk in the spirit not to for fill the lust of her flesh because it was one thing she knew for sure: she wanted to hold to the statues of the Word of God and to keep God's commandments. You see she knew it was nothing but the hand of God on her life and God had truly given her life and favor that no man could steal the glory from. She wasn't going to take down; you see when she was in the world she lived hard and stood strong in her evil and wicked ways. But now that she'd been freed from bondage and no longer bound by generational curses or demonic spirits; she was going to stand having done all to stand. She let go of everything in her life that was not of God and she did mean everything. She made up in her mind that no demon in hell was going to separate her from the love of God and the super-natural transformation that God had performed on her and in her. Let me help you to better understand. She is a bonafide fighter and failure is not an option. She's more than a conqueror because God told her in the Word that greater is he that is within me than he that is in the world and she believed it. Because according to her earnest expectations and her hope that in nothing shall she be ashamed but that with all boldness as always so now Christ shall be magnified in her body, whether it be by life or by death. For to her to live is Christ and to die is gain. You see she meant business when it came to her salvation. She was once blind and while living a life of sin she walked as those of the world but now through the power of the Holy Ghost she's been made free and separate from sin. For if we live in the spirit let us also walk in the spirit. People of God it's imperative that you understand the importance of your salvation as a Child of God. It's a personal walk and a lonesome road in which strait is the gate and narrow is the way which leadeth unto life and few there be that find it. Now ask yourself. Have I entered the wrong gate? Stop being a people pleaser and pick up your cross and bare it to the glory of God. Think of the grace, mercy, longsuffering, loving kindness and compassion your Lord and Savior Jesus Christ has for you. Do you know that Jesus hung bleed and died for our sins? Jesus fought the ultimate fight for all of us which was Satan taking the keys to death, hell and the grave. Have you caught the revelation yet? The battle is already won; all you have to do is live Holy and apply the Word of God in every aspect of your life. (Galatians 5:1) Stand fast therefore in the liberty wherewith Christ hath made us free, and be not entangled again with the yoke of bondage. God told you that he gave you power. (Luke 10:19) Behold, I give unto you power to tread over serpents and scorpions, and over all the power of the enemy: and nothing shall by any means hurt you. This is a Word to the Wise no Holy Ghost no Power! People of God without the Holy Ghost you have no power you are just like the sons of sceva. That's why it's so important to not just carry the Bible but to read the Bible and retain it that you may be filled with all the knowledge of God. Did you know that when you are freed from the bondage of the world you gain peace? So stop allowing Satan to play baton mitten with your soul and for the love of Christ don't die with a religious spirit or self-righteous spirit and be cast into hell. Let it not be said unto you, ye did run well; who did hinder you that ye should not obey the truth? Don't allow Satan to cause you to become your own worst enemy. For how can you believe in God and deny the power thereof? When you see the hand of God on a person's life that you know was once bound and they are now free. If you say you are a Child of God instead of discouraging someone with the things you just read pertaining to the experiences of her christian walk. You should now begin to encourage them by giving God the honor and the glory for the marvelous transformation in their life. Try this self-examination. If the unsaved her use to run with us in uncleanness, fornication and drunkenness all which are the works manifested in the flesh in which no man who partake of shall inherit the kingdom of God. Yet now God has delivered, saved and sanctified her through the Holy Ghost which is now evident in her life. She has been plucked out and far removed, yet we are still coop together indulging in sin. It's now time to pop the big question to yourself; do I really have God in my life? Am I really truly saved? Do I have the Holy Ghost dwelling within me? Or am I reprobate? Do I have strong delusion? If you found yourself in this scenario I say to you stop allowing Satan to cause you to era in your mind. The truth is simple if you defy the Word of God then you're not a Child of God you are a Child of Belial. This is a Word to the Wise God is not at your card parties, nor is God in the mist of your sins and above all God will never tempt you to sin. This is one of the biggest tricks of the enemy so be not deceived any longer for it's not too late and with the breathe you have right now. You could ask God to forgive you of your trespasses as you forgive those who trespass against you. Turn from your wicked ways and sin no more lean not to your own understanding but trust in the Lord and he shall direct your paths. For it is through the paradigm shift of her life that she gained a greater understanding by faith in knowing that God wouldn't allow her enemies to wrongfully rejoice over her. She knew beyond a shadow of a doubt that God wouldn't let her enemies triumph over her. For the Bible say's (Psalm 37:17) For the arms of the wicked shall be broken: but the Lord upholdeth the righteous. And she believed the Word of God to the saving of her soul. Did you know that the fear of God is the beginning of wisdom? How can you hear the Word without a preacher? How can he preach except he be sent? This is why it's important that we make sure that a Man of God is chosen and sent of God.

You have to try the spirit by the spirit to see whether it's of God having the understanding that God will never say anything contrary to his word. A true Man of God or Woman of God will never deviate from the Word of God. For instance a true shepherd will never tell you that homosexuality is of God and acceptable to God. Although God love those that are bound by this transgression God hates the sin. That's why it's important to examine yourself and know that you have the true spirit of God. It's just like a baby certain formulas will cause them to spit up but the right formula will digest. What formula are you on? Which reminds her of the unsaved her in years prior. (Remember you're on the quiet storm and the turns will twist your understanding) You see one day in passing a Man of God said to her "I'm from a world that you know nothing of." It was as if a light-bulb had been immediately turned on in her unsaved head as she replied. Wait a minute. If there's a world inside this world that I know nothing of I want to know it and from that moment she began to hunger and thirst after righteousness. You see the unsaved her thought she knew everything just because she had done just about everything the world had to offer, so to speak. From lavish vacations, exotic foods, luxury cars, fine jewelry, flaming liquor, best of designer clothes, mink coats, shoes, hand bags and much more then she cares to name. Need she mention dirty money, she'd partied with the upper class so to speak, socialized with business men, politician, lawmen, so called preachers and the list goes on. In other words the unsaved her had engaged the minds of many and she didn't long for anything. The unsaved her was a force to be reckoned with, a terror, bold, arrogant, nasty, rude, controlling and most of all heartless. The unsaved her wouldn't allow any man to rule over her, she had a true jezebel spirit; she was ruthless, opinionated, she rowed her own boat, she was a free spirit, daring, cold-blooded, fearless and headed to an early grave and a burning hell! You see the spirit that lied within her was so powerful and intimidating it would paralyze those in its presence, it thrived off the fear of others as it grew stronger and stronger. This spirit within her was untamable, voice stress, stuck-up and cruel. As she would strut her banging body, slinging her beautiful long flowing hair that wasn't store bought and nails naturally long like animal claws. She kept herself up as she was decked out with diamonds, smelling rich and riding slick and that's not even the half of her unsaved story beacuse if you knew it all you would need smelling salts. She thought she knew God just because she went to church here and there. Just like some of you who are reading a Word to the Wise. Then all of a sudden out of nowhere she was enlightened she had a spiritual experience that she couldn't explain. It was just a simple statement "I'm from a world that you know nothing of" that statement made to her by that Man of God changed her entire life. On that day she became a newborn babe desiring the sincere milk of the Word of God. Truly I say to you her life had taken a three-hundred and sixty degree turn on that day. In other words on that day the rubber meet the road. You see she had finally found the true formula out of life's many mixes and although she was yet a sinner, she was able to discern the truth. Did you know there are many formulas (Doctrine's) in the church world? Her experience allowed her to taste the true spirit of God. Ask yourself are you feed by a false prophet or a true Man of God or Woman of God? She was broking to tears just thinking of how God loved her and despite her innumerous iniquity, God had mercy on her. You see only God could perform a transformation such as she'd become. You see she had suffered some traumatic experiences in life which caused her to become heartless and cold-blooded toward men. She needed to be healed from all the sexual abuse that she had suffered through-out her entire life. She was a battered woman and as a child she had her innocence physically stolen. Which left her mentally shattered, hopeless and unable to trust. For ten long years she prayed this prayer. God send me a love and allow me to love. I tell you not only did God send her a love he topped it off in the form of a Man of God. She had no clue that the Man of God in passing would become her husband she never saw it coming. She was so grateful to God for blessing her with such a knowledgeable, wise and understanding Man of God who prayed her through and spiritually feed her. She could only imagine her husband's private thoughts. Lord is this the one? Lord is this my punishment? God she's a ruff one! God please don't let me make a mistake. Can a woman like this be trusted? You see these were some of the many stumbling blocks in which satan placed before her to destroy her life. Now as she looks back it amazes her how the enemy tried to steal her time with roadblocks to derail her through the past trials of her life. There was times through-out her deliverance when she would reminisce back on her grammar school days. She was a straight A student with an F in conduct because she was hyper, impatient, always running ahead, couldn't sit still and wouldn't obey. She could hear her husband saying "you going to sit here until I finish and until you learn not to cut me off in the middle of my flow." I bet you were a bad little girl in school can't you hold your tongue? Ok, ok she would reply. You keep saying ok but you still not getting it. How small a thing that has so much power. The tongue is a little member and boasteth great things. Behold how great a matter a little fire kindleth! (James; 6,8) And the tongue is a fire, a world of iniquity: so is the tongue among our members, that it defileth the whole body, and setteth on fire the course of nature; and it is set on fire of hell. But the tongue can no man tame; it is an unruly evil, full of deadly poison in which it takes the power of God to tame. She can laugh about it now because she finally got her breakthrough. You see the residues of the old woman meaning the unsaved me had to be washed away and contrary to what people believe. It's not like a fairytale you can't just click your heels and everything becomes peachy keen. Salvation is free but it takes work to maintain it. Let her give you an example. While working she had an experience with a First Lady that left her baffled. After being relieved from her shift she was confronted as the First Lady rushed toward her aggressively while smoking her cigarette and rudely blowing the smoke in her face. As profanity spewed out of her mouth (Yes! A first lady) she proceeded to accuse her of something that she didn't do. She responded first lady you have the wrong person as she began to head toward the training room. You see there was a time in her unsaved life that she would've cleaned the street with that first lady but instead she brought her flesh under subjection. (Thank God for the Holy Ghost) This was supposed to be a Woman of God but thank God that whatever formula she was being feed wasn't the same formula the saved me was being feed. Here's another example. She moved out of state and the lord blessed her with a very wise beautician who's well skilled and very informed. One day after getting her hair done she had another experience with a Woman of God. She was excited to see the Woman of God and when she reached out to greet the Woman of God; the Woman of God treated her like she had the plague. The Woman of God didn't want to touch her hand but she was persistent because she needed to know beyond a shadow of a doubt that what was happening was actually happening. It was at that precise moment that her beautician obviously saw what was transpiring and spoke out saying "you got it and I'm still trying to get there. I still got a little ghetto in me" you handle yourself very well as she came from behind the chair to give her a hug. While saying how she enjoys when I come to get my hair done because she know that she's going to have some church. Now don't get the saved her wrong her beautician love her some Jesus she just keeps its one-hundred. It was obvious that this Woman of God had become infested with seeds of discord pertaining to the saved me testifying about how God delivered the unsaved me. How many of you know that some Men of God and Women of God will tell you what you can and cannot testify about? Have you experienced this sort of psychological manipulation or social influence within the church? You see just a few weeks earlier we were all sitting down together at a late dinner fellowshipping with one another and all was well. The saved her learned through her deliverance that the enemy will try to use situations or any vessel that gives way to his evil impressions to try and cause her flesh to rare up. But she thank and praise God because the formula she's on teaches her to love and not judge. That's why it's important that you are not only saved but saved and delivered. She learned that the enemy can use anyone to try to get you in your flesh even Jesus had twelve disciples and one of them was influenced by Satan. If we go by this number out of every twelve christians one is used by the enemy. So she purposed in her heart to abide by the Word of God and hold her tongue so that she's not that one out of twelve. This is why the Bible states we should examine ourselves. Did you know that people take communion every first Sunday or as often as there Pastor chooses without examining themselves? The Bible says that for this cause many are weak and sickly among you and many sleep? The Word of God says taking communion unworthily will bring damnation in your life. It's time to get right church and prepare yourself for our Lord and Savior Jesus Christ who's soon to come. People of God stop trying to reword the Bible and see yourself; it's not the Word of God that's wrong; it's all of you who won't to justify your sin. Can not your taste discern perverse or bitter things? I'm here to tell you that you can live free and separate from sin. So people of God let us go on to perfection and remember demonic spirits are real. Spot check. How can you be Holy Ghost filled if everyone in your inner circle is unsaved? What about some of you so called artist who prostitute your gift by running from church to church, like a bull out a stall seeking fame and fortune yet you say you love God. When the truth is you love money and you use God. The same goes for the organist, drummer and the guitar player. You played for free while you developed your skills in the very same church that you now charge the pastor to play in and as soon as a bigger offer is presented you forget about God for money. I've found that when you truly love God you'll desire to be used by God at whatever capacity necessary that souls may be saved and freed from bondage. Question. Why is it that some people look for friends everywhere they go? And why is it that all the friends they accumulate are trouble? Yet they can't see themselves as trouble. When did the house of God become a social club or the new happy hour? And in some cases a comedy show where the false prophet is no more than a comedian putting on a show for the congregation. It amazes the saved me to see how some of these mega churches have the Pastor bound up and afraid to preach the pure unadulterated Word of God. You tell me. How can a church have no standard if God has a standard? Have you ever wondered why your pastor avoids certain books in the Bible? These are just thought provoking questions they're not up for debate unless you have the spirit of debate and need some deliverance. People of God when did it become ok for a Man or Woman of God to except everything and anything in the House of God just to fill the seats? Ask yourself do my Pastor preach the truth concerning sin or is he or she fattening their own pockets at the expense of my soul? This is a Word to the Wise God didn't save you to be stupid! People of God can't you see that some churches have now become a place of entertainment? After you've been mesmerized by the painted faces, comedy, poetry, line dancers and the mini concert you're so worked up off your emotions that you're unaware of how you've been in church for two or more hours, yet you only heard twenty minutes of the Word of God from a Pastor who can't feed you the truth because the minute he or she begins to preach on sin the seats will empty. What a harsh reality it is to know that the preacher can't preach on homo-sexuality because of the choir director or deacon so and so. The preacher can't preach on shacking or babies out of wedlock because it will shine a light on their own childrens lifestyle and on the lifestyle of the Man or Woman of God because in some cases the child that the Man of God or Woman of God had was a product of the adultery they themselves committed as that child grows up in the church unaware in some cases that the pastor is their real father and in some cases the wife don't know that the choir member second row to the left is the mother of her husband's child and her husband deacon number five don't know that the Man of God who he loves, respects, opens doors for, brings water to, shakes his hand with a monetary blessing and also carries his Bible is his sons true father. Yep you just read that and yep I wasn't afraid to tell the truth and shame the devil. Poor pastor can't teach or preach on modest apparel when his first lady is sitting in the pull-pit with her bare arms, skinny leg blue jeans on and her legs crossed dangling her five inch heels. Talk about a Man of God being bound up. Here's a perfect example. The preacher can't even talk about something as simple as a woman's hair being her crown and glory when evangelist sip and tip got her hair bobbed off and dyed fire red. (You can close your mouth now) Let's not leave out the ushers, the choir and as quiet as it's kept the mother's board to. How can the preacher even preach on defiling your temple when he himself is standing outside the House of God smoking with the members? Ok. I get it you belong to a denomination that indulges in these sinful things and tells you that there's a mansion in Heaven for you. (Remember you're on the quiet storm and you're riding through a dark tunnel) I'm not done yet. How can the Preacher preach on drinking when he at your wedding drinking liquor too? Need I say more? Yet there is one topic that these Preachers never fail to preach on. You guessed it. Your tithes and offerings. Surely the false prophet knows how to persuade you to buy a blessing from God and some even sale prophecies to you feeble minded. She's married to a pastor who's a true Man of God and she's seen the balance of right from wrong as she listens to him rightly divide the Word of truth. He's a pastor who preaches with no respect of person whether its sin, faith or sound doctrine. This Man of God serves you the whole roll and I pray that you will find a Shepherd like him; they're out there if you seek God to find one. Yes the false prophet will pay for their deceitfulness but will it come at the expense of your soul? People of God beware because a lot of churches are filled to the brim with familiar spirits. Question. How can someone come along in twenty-twenty and tell you that God created a third gender? Or maybe the bigger question is how could you believe that? Where has anyone read in the Bible that God created a third gender? And further more if you know that homo-sexuality is ungodly, than tell me why would you sit under a false prophet that will teach you differently? How can a heterosexual person sit under a preacher that's homo-sexual and be feed? When the Word of God says how can two walk together accept they first be agreed. This is just a thought. Do you think that some of the billionaires and millionaires of the world would give to these mega churches if the Pastors preached on sin? How about this as food for thought. Sense when can anyone just walk into the pull-pit and lay hands on a Man of God? I'll answer this one: that's what money and the love thereof can do. Do you see how powerful some spirits are and how quickly one can become subject to another? The Bible states in (Mark 3:27) No man can enter into a strong man's house, and spoil his goods, except he will first bind the strong man; and then he will spoil his house. People of God you must know that God will never tempt you to sin. Remember Jesus was lead into the wilderness to be tempted of satan not God. That's why it's so important that you allow the Word of God to dwell within you that you may not believe a lie and be damned. She can tell you from her personal trial you see when she gave her life to God and began to live a life of righteousness; she experienced the greatest trials of her life. When the unsaved her was bound in sin and influenced by demonic spirits everything was excepted and acceptable. Child you only get one life you better live it to the fullest, girl you should try everything at least once, girl you better live while you can, God will call you when he ready for you. Look at the different seeds of corruption that were planted in the unsaved her. I'm not done. Girl those saved folks forgot they were once young, things are different in our generation, man yawl behind times, that's old school, this is a new day and the number one seed planted within the unsaved her was it don't take all that to be saved. If you are guilty of planting these seeds within someone it's time to stop allowing Satan to use you. And if any of those seeds that were planted within the unsaved her have burst within you, you need to cast them into the dry places where they belong. How is it that the unsaved me who was in bondage was so loved but as soon as the unsaved me became saved sanctified and filled with the Holy Ghost she was now the devil? Explain to me how can someone who fornicates and defiles their temple by smoking, drinking, drugging, stealing, shacking up, gambling and are full of corrupt communication say they're a Child of God? Yet these same so called Children of God will tell those who are now free from sin that you're crazy in religion and the Preacher has brained washed them. Let's not leave out the self-righteous and religious spirit who are far worse than the unsaved. These are those of you In whom satan has tricked through your criticism of what others have been delivered from and by only excepting those whom you deem acceptable according to the level of sin they committed. These are those so called saints and in some cases even Men of God and Women of God who become stumbling blocks for babes who are sincerely seeking to reach God. Whereby they now as the saved have unforgiveness in their own hearts and are now themselves found in need of deliverance. We must always remember that none of us are above God and God is love. That's why it's so important to read the Bible for ourselves that we may know the whole truth. You see some Pastor's steer away from certain biblical stories so they won't offend anyone or be put in a position to defend themselves. This is a Word to the Wise you must fire sin and employ righteousness and whatever you do don't give sin his job back. Question. Did you know that living a life of holiness isn't hard? All you have to do is believe the Word of God to the saving of your soul. It all boils down to you just have to want God you have to be sick and tired of being sick and tired. She learned through her deliverance that the real battle comes when you take a stand and begin to obey the Word of God in its entirety. You see when you step off satan's turf and unequivocally give your life to God and begin to fight your own good fight of faith thats when your breaking point comes. She was delivered from alcoholism, smoking, vulgarity, gambling and many more ungodly things. So she began to cleanse herself from all filthiness of the flesh out of obedience to the Word of God and as a result she was ridiculed and I do mean ridiculed! She couldn't understand how living for God caused so much hatred toward her but she gained strength through the Word of God. The Bible states in (2 Corinthians 6:17-18) Wherefore come out from among them, and be ye seperate, saith the Lord, and touch not the unclean thing; and I will recieve you, and will be a Father unto you, and ye shall be my sons and daughters, saith the Lord Almighty. By faith trust and her belief in the Word of God she continually press forward by replacing her once corrupt lifestyle with a closer intimate relationship with God. In other words she replaced her worldly sinful life with Godly things. You see she meant business when it came to her salvation "For it's everything to her" even at the expense of losing everything and everyone. You see when she was lost in a world of sin hopeless, helpless, careless and suicidal; it was God who heard her despair. She was a lost soul and Satan was having his way with her; her entire life was sex, drugs, partying, deceiving and money. The unsaved her lived to show out, she thrived off of hurting others, she was full of spirits that entered her at a young age and she was torn inside from a life of sexual abuse. Her life was filled with countless memories that played like a broken record in her mind as she was hell bent on paying back men for the torture that gripped her soul. The saved her understands when the scripture (1 Corinthians 6:11) says but ye are washed, but ye are sanctified, but ye are justified in the name of the Lord Jesus, and by the Spirit of our God. This is A Word to the Wise you must be born again and washed by the blood of the lamb. She was blood washed, born again, saved, sanctified and now she's living a life conducive to Gods perfect will for her life. Did you know that the Word of God applies to everybody? Yes. That means you and the unbeliever to. That's why it's important to have a personal relationship with God and possess the power of the Holy Ghost within you that you may resist the wiles of the devil. People of God no Holy Ghost no power. The Word of God is a lamp unto your feet, and a light unto your path it's the guide that leads you to salvation. You must remember there will always be trials of life but they come to make you strong. Just as the Word of God say's weeping may endure for a night but joy comes in the morning your devil free season will come. She's reminded of a trial she faced you see the enemy is always trying to break you down and cause you to doubt God. You see his paradigm shift involved her which brought forth a change in her life as she recieved her heart's desire; but it would also cause her to reinvent herself so to speak. You see she worked for the city and after nineteen consecutive years of employment, she would now have the experience of being unemployed. She went from $2500 plus after taxes bi-weekly to living by faith. One day she was sitting on the loveseat and she hollered! Honey, I want to be a pharmacist technician. Her husband replied. Ok sweetheart that fits you. Three weeks later she found a school which was only about a forty minute drive from her home. It was perfect because not only would she be licensed in one state; she would also be licensed in two states which was awesome and would also open up so many more opportunities for her. She was scheduled an interview where she had to pass a test in order to be excepted into the program. The test consisted of fifty various questions in which she had three minutes to answer as many as she could. To God be the glory she passed the test. I'm telling you everything was flawless, not only was she excepted into the pharmacy technician program a door opened and a $14,000 financial blessing was poured out. There was only one thing the school had to do and that was send out for her high school transcripts. Everything was taken care of from her uniforms down to the books and her first day of class was scheduled for 8:45am September twenty-third. Her schedule was Monday thru Thursday 8:45am to 1:30pm and after the successful completion of every course she would have her license in nine months. She was so excited as she could really see this career fitting her. Wow. Not only had her life changed as she had been given her hearts desire she was now blessed with a new career all within the first two months of her transition. I'm telling you God is so awesome he can do anything but fail. She's reminded of how two months prior to the paradigm shift she would cry out to God through prayer asking God to just bless them she would tell God how she trusted him and that she had placed them in the palm of his hand. Because she understood that God just allowed her to be a part of their life but ultimately they belonged to him. She would tell God that she knew he would make a way for them because they were his and by faith she believed and God did just that. The Man of God and her would always discuss taking a road trip yet they had no idea it would come in this fashion. God is her all and all and now her faith has been put in action because she no longer had a paycheck to depend on. As she followed the spiritual bread crumbs of Jesus with the understanding of what it truly means when the scripture say's the just shall live by faith. Her phone rings it about 9:30am she answers hello, the caller replies hello how are you today? I'm doing just wonderfully and yourself? I'm ok. I'm sorry to have to call you this is the administrative office. Yes she responded. The person on the other end of the phone begins to say "I'm sorry to say but in the process of requesting your transcripts we were informed that the school you attended (at the same time she was speaking in my left ear a voice said to me remember my promises to you) was fraudulent. She responded ma'am; she couldn't believe what she was hearing as the person on the other end of the phone said I'm sorry I know this is devastating news. As they began to give her the information needed to follow up for herself. They couldn't stop saying how sorry they were to deliver such horrific news to me and how it meant that I couldn't attend the pharmacy technician program. Her words to the person on the other end of the telephone were it is well. God is going to get the glory out of this as her heart dropped. By now her husband is saying sweetheart what's going on? With her head in her hands she briefly explained the phone conversation and he froze in disbelief. Honey they gave me a number to call so that I may get a greater understanding concerning the situation. Hello. hello she responded I'm calling to inquire about receiving a copy of my transcripts? People of God when you're faced with a challenging situation don't react emotionally but remember you have God on your side. She graduated from a private school, she obtained her nursing license and worked as a Hospice nurse for nearly seven years.

Talk about a heavy load. The Man of God reached out to embraced her saying "everything will be alright sweetheart" you have to just keep going and remember you're an author; put this in your book. She looked up at him and smiled saying "it is well." This was a job for Jesus. You see some how deep down inside of her, she felt as though this was by design and we know all things work together for good to them that love God to them that are called according to his purpose. She knew that the enemy would love for her to break, waiver and doubt her God after being dealt such a horrible blow. But instead she looked at her trial as only a test of her faith and by no means would she let her faith fell or her God down. (Proverbs 3:5-6) Trust in the lord with all thine heart; and lean not unto thine own understanding. In all thy ways acknowledge him, and he shall direct thy paths. If God promised you something, it will come to pass, for he is faithful that promised. She recognized that at the same time the enemy was trying to break her, God was bringing her into remembrance of his promise to her. She learned that trials don't cease once you become born again in actuality they become greater because of the change in your lifestyle. This is a Word to the Wise stop giving up on God through disbelief. If God has promised you something then surely he shall bring it to pass in your life. People of God stop allowing the enemy to defeat you. It's time to get rid of the why's and why not's of your life. What gives you the right to put God on a time limit? Is this you? Well if it don't happen by next year this time it's not meant for me. If I'm not married by such and such age then God don't want me to be married. If I don't get pregnant by the time I'm forty I guess I'll never get pregnant. Or maybe you're guilty of throwing a pity party. Why did my father/mother give me away yet they kept my brothers and sisters? Why did my husband/wife commit adultery? Why is my son/daughter strong out on dope? Why didn't I get the promotion? Why don't I have a new car? Why did all those bad things happen to me as a child? Why has my life been one failure after another? Why wasn't I loved? Why, why, why, why, why sound like the cry of a newborn baby. Why not you? Just think about it for a second......whatever you've suffered in your personal life it has no comparison to what Jesus endured and Jesus didn't complain or murmur. Instead Jesus said to his father not my will but thine will be done. People of God through spiritual maturity the saved me found comfort, peace and freedom within my mind, body and soul through Jesus Christ who became the ultimate sacrifice for me. People of God we all have suffered some things in which some people are too ashamed to speak of but the saved me will not allow the enemy to suffocate the miracles that God have performed in my life. For there is truly nothing new under the sun and if you read your Bible you'll see that the gruesome things that you've suffered were suffered by some biblically as well. So the shame is no longer on the saved me it's on all you so called christians who now judge the saved me based on the sins the unsaved me was delivered from. Yes she told her testimony and yes she's bold but her boldness is in Christ Jesus and all to the Glory of God. So to put your mouth on the saved her is to put your mouth on a work of God because her mind is like finished concrete thoroughly mixed and permanently set. This is a Word to the Wise it's time to stop your worldly way of living and get rid of your stinking thinking. You must resist the relationship with the adversary by letting go and allowing God to do the God thing in every area of your life. Did you know that just because you have a great big house, fancy designer clothes and you're riding luxuriously doesn't mean that you're blessed and highly favored? That's why it's important to know who your master is because Satan gives gifts to. Truth be told some of you so called christians pulling into the church parking lot in your luxury cars, wearing your Sunday best got it because you rolled the dice or bartered yourself. Yep! That scratch card, lottery ticket, one arm bandit or was it your favorite horse, or maybe your sugar daddy/sugar momma bought it for you. You tell me how can you fix your mouth to say God blessed you when it came from the devil by way of sin? Let me give you another example. Some of you come out the church house anointed and gifted in singing yet that's not satisfying enough for you. So you crossover claiming it's just to make a name for yourself and you say that once you become established you're going to return to the Church House. But everyone knows the real reason you're leaving the church is so you can become recognized and financially stable. Has it ever crossed your mind that it wasn't the Church you left? Was God not good enough for you? How could you look pass God and choose Satan as your provider? Don't you know that God created all things? Can you imagine the countless souls that have gone to hell using this very same formula? Did you know that you can leave God and never find your way back? Just think about it for a moment some people do it to death. You may laugh but it's the truth some become famous straight to hell. Remember satan was a masterful musician and demonic spirits are real. Now ask yourself if God has the power over all things then why would I choose to serve anything less than God? In other words why do you choose to be cursed rather than blessed? Let me make it plain. Heaven is before you and you've been told that in heaven there will be no more death, sickness, or sorrow yet you choose hell because your flesh likes thrills and mystery. Ok I'll make it plainer some of you can't resist that married man or woman you just got to have what belongs to someone else but you'll do life in prison if someone touches yours. You still didn't get it? You'll murder someone else's child without regard but when it comes to your child life matters. Question. Do you think Satan is going to let you steal from his world to better yourself in Gods world? The Word of God clearly states choose this day whom ye will serve. Don't you know that satan is the father of all lies, a masterful deceiver, murderer, thief and destroyer? People of God how could you allow such a thought of foolery to be implanted in your brain and sealed in your heart? Is it because you love the world and the glitz and glamour thereof? Maybe you want instant gratification in exchange for eternal damnation? Let me enlighten you. The truth is with all you have and all you due whether it be sailing the seven seas, eating the finest foods, driving the latest and greatest vehicle, decked out in your fancy array and choosing your nightly dessert. You'll still never find satisfaction as you become restless and wanton deceiving and being deceived. Your money; even for thoughs of you that are filthy rich will never fill the void in your heart. I'm referring to that emptiness that just won't go away; you see that's a pain she know all to well. You've tried counseling, psychiatrists and medication. Alcohol won't take the pain away, drugs won't take the pain away, food don't take the pain away, sex can't heal the pains, not even shopping. These are overwhelming fleshly desires influenced by spiritual wickedness as each day you awake and put on your daily mask. While the people that you think truly love you watch you bleed out slowly as they tell you everything they possibly can to comfort you just so they can keep their palms greased. Is it that you're too blind to see the demonic influences in your life or is the temptation of sin too great for you to resist? Truth be told the only thing that can stop the hemorrhage of your life is God. This is a Word to the Wise while you still have breathe in your body you can leave that broadway that leads to destruction and enter the narrow way that leads to life. For what does it prophet a man to gain the whole world and lose his soul? You've tried everything else so why not try Jesus? You see by faith she was delivered from a world of sin. She was freed from the prison of her mind; she was healed from sexual abuse, mental abuse, physical abuse and lack of love. All these things plus more tormented the unsaved her but through her deliverance they were washed away by the blood of Jesus Christ which can make the vilest sinner clean. The saved her forgave the unsaved her for the many ungodly sins that the unsaved her had committed as the saved her found love, peace and joy over in the Holy Ghost. The saved her will admit that coming through her personal deliverance of prescription pills, alcoholism, adultery, gambling, cursing, vanity and the list goes on and on was nothing compared to being delivered from her inner circle and most of all the pleasure of sin in the world. She found for herself that Gods Word is real and it's alive. "If any man be in Christ he's a new creature." It wasn't until she became born again and took her stand in

God that she truly saw what she meant to others. Although they saw the transformation in her life they refused to believe it and couldn't except the truth which was God had truly got ahold to her. Instead they over looked the power and presence of God in her life by lashing out at the Man of God in whom God used not only to teach her the Word of God but to feed her the whole truth according to the Word of God. She couldn't believe how they blamed the very Man of God that prayed her through a man who despite her past reputation yet trusted God and out of his obedience, faith and determination she was set free from the generational curses of her bloodline. It amazed her to see how so many people including some of the church folk could only see man and not the hand of God threw her deliverance. Remember you're riding the quiet storm so hold on to your wigs because the speed is about to increase as we get into the self-righteous who tried to assassinate the saved her as they were used by demonic spirits and unaware until now. (Deliver Lord) Enough already this has now gone on long enough as they would call and say to the saved me. You have allowed this man to brain wash you as she would break in with a trembling voice saying "how could this be wrong?" I know longer drink and run around in the street why aren't you happy for me? I'm still me I'm just a saved me with tears streaming down her face as she woud ask them why are you giving me an ultimatum? How could you place me in a position to choose between God and you? I have nothing to talk to you about I don't know you anymore as they would hang up the phone. Can you believe until this very day they still feel as though I walked out of their lives? They always say you don't know where you're going but you know where you've been. Before hanging up the phone the saved me would always say to them "whenever you think of me remember I'm safe because I'm now in God." As they would reply. "Whatever you wrong" as they hung up the phone. I know I've repeated these conversations throughout the book but I'm painting a picture. She don't have any good memories with them sense God has delivered her; she only have the memories of pain and sorrow. She can't tell you what it feels like to have their arms around her. There have been times that she was broken and only the arms of a mother could soothe the pain or take the fear away. She can't tell you the countless times she cried to the Man of God wondering if she would ever fill their arms around her again or would she ever be able to see their smile and hear their laugh again. She needed them to help encourage her through her deliverance, she needed them to comfort her and assure her, she needed them to believe in her and tell her that everything was going to be alright. She needed them to be proud to tell the world how God blessed me and brought me from a horrible pit. She needed a praying person that understood her deliverance and how it allowed her to become free from bondage as it broke every chain of the generational curses off of her life. She suffered gravely and it wasn't in silence because she cried out loud every day so much so that most times she cried herself to sleep. And then she woke up in the morning and cried herself to work I tell you she cried, she cried and then she cried some more. But there was one thing she understood for sure; she wasn't going to compromise the Word of God. And by the way the self-righteous didn't love the God in her either. If you think they were cold toward the saved me it was nothing compared to some of the so called first ladies. Yes. First Ladies/Women of God. You and your congregation know exactly who you are. You sanctified women who were not only cold-blooded toward the saved me you were heartless and ruthless with your bullying. As the Men of God/Husband's said nothing as their Jezebel exposed the Ahab within them. Truth be told if you would've met the unsaved her; she would've tasted your husband and took your seat. I said it! The quiet storm is picking up speed now as we go into a triple loop. Tell the truth and shame the devil or the tornado in ____eels who has one foot in the grave and the other on a banana peel. God see's you social media queen who's in need of deliverance. Yes. she said it and I screen shot it to. I saw that seven letter word you posted; that word may be in the bible but you didn't use it in that content you used it as a curse word as it was pertaining to politics and your members saw it as they overlook your backslidden state. She not trying to hurt you she trying to help you by saying the things that need to be said that you may get some deliverance before your hour come. Through deliverance the saved me learned that she wasn't loved she was excepted only because of what she could do or the attention she drew when she was in the world. The people she was surrounded by enjoyed the thrill and the element of surprise she provided whenever she would grace them with her presence. She sometimes wondered if they only wanted her around because of the free drinks in the night club or money that was given to her because some wealthy man felt as though she was good luck while she was standing at the poker table. It could've been a number of things that she care not to disclose that kept the relationships. These people were never real friends and now she clearly see that they were no more than opportunists. Truth be told if you stab your sister in the back what would you do to someone that's not your blood? It's amazing once the scales fall off your eyes how clearly those of us who were once blind now see. I'm telling you the sky has never been bluer neither has the grass been greener. She can honestly say she didn't get any support and they know exactly who they are seeming as though she was closer to them than her very own inner circle. Would you like her to share the consolation prize that she received from all those in which she just spoke of? Simply nothing from some, others gave her you wrong, how could you let that man isolate you? I don't know how to take you anymore and my number one prize was you've become a stranger to us now. How could anyone say such a thing to a person that has been in their life for over thirty years? So everyone buried her. And though she live, she yet died, which allows her to say, she know how life would have gone on after her death, even though she's still alive. Being born again has giving her the total experience of how old things pass away and all things become new. To God be all the glory you see Gods chemical laboratory of redemption is an undeniable, supernatural, personal one on one surgery that only God himself can perform. Man can steal no Glory from God when it comes to the power of the Holy Ghost. Just as man can't explain that special place in everyone's heart that nothing passes through. How perplexing is such a thing as the human brain? People of God when you truly have the experience of Gods Holy Ghost power. You'll give the very breathe in your body before you will allow anyone or anything to cause you to denounce, deny, debate or doubt Gods supernatural ability to heal deliver and set free. With that being said explain to me how so many of you so called christians have become uplifted? So many of you christians have now fallen into the enemy's trap of self-righteousness which has caused you to enter into a spirit of era. How can a Man of God or Woman of God put their mouth on God's deliverance? How can a Man of God or Woman of God preach hard core sin and deliverance yet they have a repugnance toward one's deliverance? Do a Man of God or Woman of God have the authority to decide what sins are forgivable or unforgivable? Has your pastor told you that he has to answer whether or not you can get into heaven? She's being very serious because she heard a Man of God say this with her very own ears and many of his members believe it. She's finding out as she navigate through the church that there are Men of God and Women of God pastoring churches and they themselves are in a backslidden state. She's also found that there are a lot of christians who are personality worshippers. They are not into God but they are wrapped up in the spirit of the Man of God or Woman of God. We can't leave out the groupies who are fascinated by the Man of God and flopping around like a chicken with their head cut off. What about these pimping preachers, who are full of themselves and using there gift to mesmerize and swindle people without the concern for their souls. People of God this is a Word to the Wise the Word of God makes you aware of all things. So if you're among an ignorant people who are no more than Bible toting false prophets and sinners you have no excuse. Be not deceived People of God gifts and callings are without repentance and remember many are called but few are chosen. We as the People of God must be able to discern the difference between a gift and Gods anointed. Every man must work out his own soul salvation with fear and trembling: all while keeping in mind that this is a personal walk and a lonesome road. Daddy can't walk it for you and mama can't walk it for you; you must pick up your own cross and bare it. People of God no man has the monopoly on God it's a daily walk and don't think for one second because you made it through certain trials, tribulation and afflictions that you have mastered your salvation. For as long as you live on this side your faith will be tested. So ask yourself. Can I find hope in unhopeful times? When my faith is failing and I'm running on empty will I trust the Word of God? Will I allow my affliction to cause me to doubt God and accept death as my outcome or will I stand on the Word of God by faith? The Bible tells us that we go from faith to faith so the faith that you use for one trial may not be enough faith for your next trial. God is raising up an army in these last and evil days. Soldiers who are sold out and willing to stand having done all to stand, a soldier that is obedient and rooted, a soldier that will not murmur and complain. God wants a Child of God that will not take down or compromise the Word of God. One who's without spot or blemish, living holy in the church, at home, at work and even in the grocery store. A Child of God whose conversation is holy and you look holy. In other words God is looking for a peculiar people a royal priesthood. This is a Word to the Wise you may be able to shuck and jive the world but you will never be able to manipulate God. Can I help somebody? God isn't your sugar daddy nor is God your rabbits foot God wants a yes when you up and when you down through all your highs and your lows. People of God in this day there is now a great fallen away so don't be found guilty for those of you who say you know Jesus. For if you're not born again you only know of Jesus. It's time to give your life over to God and refuse to let the devil put you on display. She learned through her own personal experience as she travel the lonesome road that some christians even though God has saved her, sanctified her, delivered her and filled her with his precious Holy Ghost, will only see the dot and not the whole picture. In other words they can't see the saved her pass what the unsaved her was delivered from. It's so very painful when even in the church arena some of the so called Men of God and Women of God choice to categorize the saved her and look pass Gods deliverance in her life. How could the so called Man of God and Woman of God look pass the Holy Ghost and attack her past sins which are under the blood of Jesus? Oh and by the way in some cases it poured over into their congregation as some of their members began to shown the saved her. Has anyone of you members ever stopped and questioned what happened to the Elder and his wife because one day they were here and then they were gone? Or did you just believe you're lieing leaders? I guess you'll have your answer on judgment day. My prayer for you is that you don't be found guilty in the cover-up. Now put yourself in the saved her shoes or better yet try to picture her husband the Man of God sitting in the pulpit as his saved wife is being constantly perniciously preached on across the pulpit as if the Man of God of the church sent the order to his wife the Woman of God to attack the saved her as if she was a lioness out for prey. This isn't a fabricated story People of God there's more up ahead. She's going to write her truth until somebody gets delivered and that demonic cockatrice spirit operating through that individual gets exposed. Can you imagine how many souls have been destroyed because of tumultuous pernicious preaching? I can only imagine how many souls that have become wounded behind this kind of cruelty. I'm talking about people of all walks of life who bleed out and were spiritually destroyed due to the pernicious preaching within that church house. Can you imagine how many christians who've become spiritually stressed with the concern of being accepted? This statement goes out to everyone; sin is sin no matter what form or fashion. She learned through her deliverance that there's an enemy to your faith seeking to cause doubt, hindrance, stumbling blocks, confusion, division, weariness, slothfulness, sorrow, depression or anything that will steal your praise and ultimately bring you to a spiritual death. Did you know that demons are assigned to your life just like you have a gaurdian angel assigned to your life? This isn't just a fairy tale. Their are also spirits that follow you through generations which are generational curses. Did you know that your spirit will take on the attribute's and characteristics of your father or mother or father's father or mother's mother and so on. These habits or curses are inspired by demonic forces that continue to keep you entrapped in this cycle. Yes I'm talking about the mulberry bush of your life that vicious repeated cycle that you continue to find yourself locked into. Yes. I'm talking about that thing that keeps you waking up in a strangers bed, you tossed those cigarettes out the window on the way home from church but three days later you were buying another pack, you repented for you're abusive behavior and you promised your wife you would'nt strike her again but three months later after sucking down them spirits you know what I'm talking about I'll just make it plain them shots you've now broken her nose, you told God if he blessed you with another house after you lost the first house because you couldn't stop hanging out with that one arm bandit that you'd never gamble again and three years later you were right back in the same situation, you're rocking that sweet little blessing after you told God you wouldn't give in to the lust of your flesh but you now have another one on the way after getting rid of two. Over and over again you find yourself right back where you started from and the scary thing is you don't miss a service when the church doors are open. This is why the scripture says in (John 8:36) If the Son therefore shall make you free, ye shall be free indeed. People of God remember this one thing you're always in spiritual warfare and Satan is real. Satan will use whatever vessel that will yield to him to destroy you. So whether you're saved or unsaved you're still in the war so don't become a casualty. This is a Word to the Wise don't allow anyone to silence your testimony! Your testimony is to the glory of God building faith in those yet bound whom through your testimony gain hope, strength and faith that they too can be freed from there bondage of sin, hurt, torment, abuse, fear, hopelessness, adultery, perversion, secrets and inner most demons. So once again People of God don't you ever allow anyone or anything to bind up your testimony. Tell it, tell how God has set you free from the demonic forces that ripped through your life and gripped your soul. It was God's grace, mercy, unmerited love and favor that brought the unsaved me out of the clutches of satan. Some of you think that the saved me told it all concerning the unsaved me but the saved me will say to you that it was the PG version, you couldn't phantom how much more there is and if the saved me told it in-depth, some of you would not only have nightmares you'd need therapy. So just for you special few who couldn't forgive the saved me for exposing my past sinful state of mind in which I was full of demonic spirits and bound by generational curses. She say's to you on this day that God has forgiven her and she's forgiven herself. She could've written her life story which would have made the most seductive authors mouths fly open because it was just that dark. But thanks be unto God who giveth her the victory she's been born again and blood washed so she wrote as clean as she possibly could with the understanding that some things can only be told a certain way. She writes praying that the bound soul will go to the altar and cast their cares upon the Lord. Why do some people try to pull your past sins out from under the blood of Jesus? Now ask yourself. Are my hands bloody? The saved me wants to know where did the love go that you first showered me with? "Woman of God you have such a beautiful spirit." You have a pure heart, along with hugs, kisses and always soliciting prayer from me. But as soon as you heard the saved me testify I became as a filthy menstraul rag that you began to preach on. She came to your ministry saved, sanctified and filled with the Holy Ghost. She didn't need deliverance and if she did God couldn't use you because you can't get pass her testimony of how God set her free from an enomorious iniquity. Some of you church folk don't have an excuse because you say out of your own mouths as you stand and testify that you've been in church and saved all your life. Well she was breaded up in a evil lifestyle; she had no one to tell her about being saved, she wasn't raised in church all her life and neither has she been saved and then backslidden as some of you have and still are in some cases. Let's just shine a little more light on those of you that testify that you've been saved all your life because to me that's a very bold statement to make when you're not married but you've given birth to three children with three different baby daddies or you've fathered a child out of wedlock. This is a Word to the Wise unrepented continual sexual intercourse is a indication that you are not saved. Fornication is sexual intercourse between people not married to each other. So quess what? If you didn't know now you know you haven't been saved all your life and satan has caused you to believe a lie. Period. What about that DUI, domestic violence case, cigarette for your nerves or porn addiction? If this is you; you haven't been saved all your life you been in church all your life. Yes, you know about Jesus but you haven't had a experience with Jesus. Question. How can you as a Man of God or Woman of God forgive your children for their whoredoms yet you can't forgive someone else? Why is the woman always labeled? What about the man with the spirit of lust within him who's willing to lose his family just to satisfy his flesh? And after the man chases the woman like a mangy dog an innocent child is born and the woman is labeled a whore and kicked out the church. What about the man? Where is the God in that? The Bible states in (John 8:7) "He that is without sin among you, let him cast a stone at her." Can you imagine how many souls have been lost due to this kind of judgmental and unforgiven ministry? How hypocritical you are; shame on you. Now think about that for a moment. If the Man of God and Woman of God preached on that type of woman they would have to preach on every woman that comes through their church door from then on out. All because they can't get pass the unforgiveness in their own heart toward this type of woman. I pray for the Man of God and Woman of Gods deliverance and above that I pray that before their demise they will see the era of their ways because the very same hell they preach and threaten others with is the very same hell they will end up in if they themselves don't repent. Did you notice how she stated their church? You see Gods church is full of people who were x-pimps, prostitutes, drug addicts, alcoholics, adultery's and so many more ungodly things in whom God has set free. This is what makes the Power of God so great. (John 8:36) If the Son therefore shall make you free, ye shall be free indeed. Man of God and Woman of God when did the Word of God stop at the leaders? How can a Pastor lead except he lead by example? Here's an example of what I mean. If I had to come out from amongst them and be separate and not have commune with darkness or sit with the workers of iniquity or fellowship with the unrighteous. Then how is it that a Man of God and Woman of God can continue their fellowship with the works of darkness? I'm listening. How can you preach to your congregation when your very own children live like the devil, show you know respect during church service and preach against you're very standard, as they talk openly about you and against you. She not hear saying she was one of the very ones that they warned concerning yawl. Yea really though she's going to write until she's set free and this is just for you. Yea you the one who told the Man of God her husband to tell her to rewrite her testimony. Don't get mad Man of God remember you saved, sanctified and Holy Ghost filled. You was bold enough to preach on the saved her and turn many against the saved her so now its time for you to take your medicine as she write and you read about yourself this time now rebuke that. You're riding the quiet storm and after this next loop the ride will reverse so hold on to your collar and make know mistake she's not angry God healed her when that demonic spirit operating through yawl tried to spiritually destroy the Jesus within the saved her. To God be all the glory because she could've become a casualty lost in the abyss of your tyrancy like so many others became. To those of you who were able to become freed from your bondage during the time the saved her was within that church I'm so grateful to God because those private conversations after service were severe but God delivered every one of and you know just who you are. Yes you banked her thousands, you swallowed her meals, you used her and abused her and swept it all under the rug with the rest of your dirty secrets but now your skirt tail is over your head and all your evilness is showing. You don't look so holy as you read the ink on these pages now do you? My, my, my but its all for your good and its truly out of my love for you. She's not the one laughing in your face allowing you to go on in your hateful, spiteful, rude and manipulative ways. How can you as a Pastor who preaches pure holiness allow anyone to minister over your congregation after being out all night partying with the world? As the evidence is plastered all over social media. The Bible say's (Romans 14:16) Let not then your good be evil spoken of and what scares me the most about all of this is that they all take communion. Answer me this. Since when did it become Preacher before God? How can a Man of God say to his congregation all yawl can leave I don't care this is my church and I'll come and worship all by myself? This isn't hear say she heard it with her very own ears as it came straight from the horse's mouth. With statements like that it didn't surprise her to see that their church was bleeding out. Something is clearly wrong when a church goes from standing room only to at best thirty people on Sunday. Talk about bondage this Man of God ruled with fear and intimidation. The saved her never seen this type of intimidation except for when she was unsaved and around pimps and gangsters. She was shocked to see the fear that came over his members and how the atmosphere changed whenever this Man of God entered a room. When this Man of God would enter the room Men of God and Women of God would go from being open and happy to closed and reserved. The atmosphere would become gloomy, quiet and stale as he would do all the talking and boy o boy could she identify with that spirit. You see some never get delivered from their mien controlling, strong arming ways it's either their way or no way. God be with the man that will challenge this spirit because when a Man of God enters a room there should be a fresh anointing and excitement not a sour smell and she means that literally. The presence of a Man of God shouldn't remind you of how you were bullied in gramma school. Not only is this Man of God a bully he's also territorial and retaliatorial and his weapon of choice is slander. She solicit your prayers for any Man of God bound by this type of spirit because they'll never have a good understanding or always feel misunderstood. That's why it's so important to stand on the Word of God without compromising or wavering because the more you sit around the ungodly the more they massage into your spirit. She understand the Pastor's family is important but when did they become more important than the souls God has entrusted the Man of God with? How can a Man of God or Woman of God preach a hard gospel to their congregation and not enforce it among their very own family? You tell me Man of God and Woman of God how can you sit your choir members down when they have babies out of wedlock? Yet you parade your great grands that were born out of wedlock? Or maybe you're guilty of totally neglecting your grandchild and treating them as if they didn't exist because they were conceived in adultery. Adultery is voluntary sexual intercourse between a married person and a person who is not his or her spouse. The saved her is asking questions that the multitudes won't. So don't get rocks in your jaws Man of God and Woman of God get your deliverance because it can come show as you read the words of truth from these pages concerning your unsanctified self. Look like to me Man of God and Woman of God your sin has found you out. Someone has to be bold enough to take a stand and expose the devil. So that someone is me Rahab Salmon. The Word of God say's how can two walk together except they first agree and be not deceived God is not in a church where there's division, jealousy and hatred. The Bible clearly states a house divided against itself cannot stand son divided against father, mother-n-law against daughter-n-law, daughter against mother. Hear me now she suffered the ultimate hatred from the so called sanctified so she not writing a story for you to read she writing from pure experience in hopes that if you yourself have suffered church hurt you too can receive your deliverance and it doesn't exclude the perpetrator. You see she know what it feels like to be severed because when God called her from darkness into the marvelous light she was faced with one of the greatest trials of her life. You guessed it. Separation. It felt as though her heart was being ripped out of her chest; she felt what seemed like the very life being sucked out of her. The only thing in this God given world she loved in whom she would have given her life for she had to seperate from. Yet in some strange way it feels like she did just that. The Bible states (Matthew 10:39) He that findeth his life shall lose it: and he that loseth his life for my sake shall find it. How painful is the loss of a mother's child? She didn't know the experience to the grave but she know it through her deliverance and she can tell you to let go of your child's hand by totally surrendering to God is on a whole nother level. Talk about a sour stomach you have no clue the pain she suffered and the abuse from the one person in whom she trusted. Who was constantly saying to the saved her the church world isn't what you think it is remember I've been there the church will never except a woman like you; you'll see. As they would repeat just you wait and see you'll be running back. Those very so called saved folks will never except a woman with a past such as yours you'll see. If you think women were jealous of you in the world the women in the church will be more jealous. As they would laugh saying "you'll see go on out there" She now through her deliverance truly understand unconditional love and forgiveness as she was literally taunted day in and day out. With words such as "I liked you before you married that preacher man; I wish I had the old you back." She can think back to the countless times they would pack their bags and leave. Sometimes for days on end as that cockatrice spirit would poison their minds by planting seeds of discord. She know how painful it feels to have your love ones come against you verbally and physically. She never thought she would ever hear the words I hate you come out the mouth of any one of her loved ones and especially towards her. She can recall the many threats and how they'd become so angry and hostile toward her. She can talk about the pain she felt when she heard curse words directed at her and all she could do was cry out to God saying "I refuse to allow the spirit of anger to move on me" instead I choose to walk in the spirit that I would not for fill the lust of my flesh. Let her make something very clear. She raised them with discipline. Yes. she's guilty of spoiling them but surely many can attest even them that she didn't spare the rod. She had that penny moment: just ask the one who bares the scar. She was no joke before God saved her and now she's made her face like flint as she stands on the Word of God. When she called their name before God as she gave them back to God with the understanding that they were never hers she truly meant business. She's no longer found guilty of loving them or anyone else above God. She said all that to say until you've gone through this sort of separation and prevailed as a Man of God or Woman of God how can you help someone else? You talking good but the Bible states in (Matthew 10:37) He that loveth father or mother more than me is not worthy of me: and he that loveth son or daughter more than me is not worthy of me. All she saw while she sat in their ministry was a Man of God and Woman of God who are bound by their own family. This is a Word to the Wise if you play with dead things you're more likely to join them. People of God never forget what God delivered you from and above all remember this one thing. You must have your own personal relationship with God with the understanding that it's a lonesome road and few there be in passing. It's only now that she's able to better understand how some people in the church caused the person that she looked up too to become discouraged and driven into a backslidden state. You see when the people in the world treat you better than some of those in the church; you tend to return to where you're most comfortable and excepted. This is a trick of the enemy in which he uses church folk in the church house to regain a soul. If you're reading this and you fell into that trap She wants you to know that the church didn't hurt you it was a demonic spirit operating through a person that hurt you. So I say return unto the Lord and never allow anyone or anything to sufficate the Jesus in your life. It wasn't solely the fact that the person she looked up to couldn't let go of their relatives, not even that they was once bound by the night life or even the cravings of drugs, married people and alcohol. It was because of unforgiveness, unacceptance, the constant whispers and gossip from the self-righteous that became their stumbling block. Now I ask you which side are you found on? I pray neither. She reminisce of times as a little girl when she would sit in the kitchen floor with pig tails in her head, decorated with perfectly ironed ribbons, a sun dress to match and of course she can't leave out her buster brown shoes as she combed the hair of her baby doll while watching them cook, clean, sing and cry. She now through her own persecution of the self-righteous understand their pain and grief. Every day she pray that God will deliver them and have mercy on their soul. She thank and praise God that he blessed her with a Man of God who's experienced and wise. A Man of God in whom God used to nurture her damaged heart with the Word of God and with love. This is a mighty Man of God who through his selflessness battled for her soul. You see she don't blame the church; you have good lawyers and bad lawyers, good dentist and bad dentist, good doctors and bad doctors, good preachers and bad preachers. This is why it's important as you navigate through the church to always remember that every man must work out his own soul salvation by never taking your eyes off Christ Jesus as you continually press toward the mark for the prize of the high calling of God in Christ Jesus. Has not being able to separate and touch not the unclean thing become your stumbling block? If so shake yourself because it's another day's journey on your lonesome road and you must be combat ready at all times. You must stay prayed up, be vigilant, put your feelings in your pocket, dust your feet off, pat yourself on the back and say I'm to tuff to break. You must be strong in the Lord knowing the greater the trial the greater your ministry. It's now time to take a stand and choose whom ye will serve People of God. Why won't you free yourself from the influences of the world that torment your soul and vex your spirit? Look at it like this. There's a snake slithering all around you at any time it could bite you but you get off on the high that comes from the thrill of danger. You're just like a junky enjoying their fix as you seek your next worldly injection from your supplier the devil. Are you one who say's I'm going to give my life to God when I reach a certain age? Do you know that the very age you speak of may never come? No man knows the day nor the hour when Christ will appear. But there's one thing we all know for sure death is imminent and hell is for a eternity.

Listen up it's time to stop playing church as you live like a heathen all week long and enjoy your rendezvous with the world. Pastor saw you because he was watching you on live as you video your sins for all the world to see. You showed everyone what the penny machine paid out to you and Pastor know he's going to get his ten percent so he chooses the money rather than deliverance for your soul. Wow! Like really though saturday night you were throwing back shots on live with a potty mouth. Then without fear of God you have the audacity to walk through the doors of the House of God and lead the choir sunday morning. Talk about the nerve of some folks. Child I'm scared of you as you speak gibberish and cut your step in the House of God. What about those of you who play that same guitar in church that you play at the juke joint? Let's not leave out those of you who curse like a sailor and then lead the prayer service or worse than that work the altar. Sweet and bitter water can't run out the same fountain, just as oil and water won't mix and neither does holy and sexy. We're living in a time now were you can't tell the difference between the church and the world because the same clothes they wear in the night club are the same clothes they wear in the church house. Where's the shame? They looking at yours and you looking at theirs. The church has become the new social hour because some Men of God and Women of God have turned away from preaching condemnation instead they stand in the pulpit and have conversation. (In some churches the pulpit has been turned into a stage. Oh, you caught that. You so smart. Yep, thats it. It's that platform your college professor stands on as he or she has conversation with the class) As they have fallen into Satans snare and have become so bound up that if they even attempt to preach on sin the church will clear out like roaches when the lights come on and I mean that literally. Now ask yourself. Why do I go to church? Seriously. Why do you go to church? Is it to socialize? Are you there because of the prestige of that particular church? Are you there to seduce the Man of God or Woman of God? Are you there just to hear the choir? Are you looking for a husband or wife? Maybe you're there to network? Or are you a hireling? Do you attend church because its just a part of your weeky routine? Do you go to church to appease your spouse? I can't answer the question for you but I go to church to praise and worship God and to receive the inspired Word of God from the anointed Man of God or Woman of God. This is a Word to the Wise the ear that hear the reproof of life abideth among the wise and it's through the preaching of the gospel that your faith is increased and it's because of the anointing that yokes are broken. There's power, deliverance, healing, and miracles in the House of God through the presence of the Holy Ghost. So People of God don't allow Satan to trick you. If you're filled with the Holy Ghost you don't smoke, drink, curse, shack, lie, fornicate, gamble and the list goes on and on. The Holy Ghost will keep you from committing sin if you want to be kept. She know for herself that it wasn't man nor herself but it was the power of the Holy Ghost that freed her from all her defilements, worldliness and ungodly sins. God has given her something worth more than silver and gold worth more than any dollar amount. She has the greatest gift for there's nothing on earth greater than the receiving of the Holy Ghost. For the Holy Ghost is priceless it knows it's way back to heaven for it is one of three that bare record in Heaven. Glory be to God. This is a Word to the Wise you're no threat to Satan without power. That's why he's able to manipulate you as you indulge in so many ungodly things. Satan isn't worried about you; his main objective is to steal your soul and as long as you're without power he's reaching around you for your children. The only thing that can back up Satan is the power of the Holy Ghost no Holy Ghost no power. Hear me loud and clear just because you go to church and you know a few scriptures that means nothing because Satan knows the Word and has a seat in the church house just like you do whether it's in the pew, the pulpit, whether you brought him with you or it could be the person sitting next to you or maybe just maybe its you. I don't understand how some of you can sit under a pastor who committed adultery divorced his wife and married balcony first row seat seven who's now your first lady or maybe your pastor has a girlfriend, a boyfriend or a child by floppy hat who's not his wife. If you're sitting under leadership like this and you know the Word of God I'm going to just ask you plainly. What's wrong with you? What do you mean whats wrong with me? Just that. What's wrong with you? Because if you can't see that something is off with that leadership then something is also off with you. Listen at Satan speaking within your mind "we all make mistakes." People of God if she just described your leadership these are things that transpire before a Man of God and Woman of God become saved sanctified and filled with Holy Ghost power. How can one lead accept by example? This is a Word to the Wise God is coming for a Holy people. Holy meaning pure, clean, blameless, spotless, sinless, faultless, perfect, uncorrupt and sanctified. Yes sir, yes ma'am God requires all that. Money can't buy you holiness and cosmetic surgery can't perfect you to a holy state of being. This is a Word to the Wise God's law will never change but people do and just in case you didn't know a two headed man is a freak show and a double minded man is unstable in all his ways. People of God beware of the laws that go against the law of God because you will suffer the consequences of your disobedience and its more than you can bare. If God destroyed Sodom and Gomorrah what makes you think he won't do the same to this rebellious stiffnecked generation. There's a great fallen away of Gods standard as the people of the world try to silence the church. Can anybody explain to me what has happened to the House of God? The things we see now in the House of God would've never been allowed in the days of old. Many martyrs have given their lives to upholding the statutes of God and now the church is caught up in a love affair with the world. People of God the nature of man will cause him to worship something; it's in his spiritual DNA, whether it's God or money. (Matthew 6:33) Seek ye first the kingdom of God, and his righteousness; and all these things shall be added unto you. Anyone who has a real relationship with Jesus Christ knows that in the mist of their deepest despair God smiled upon them and heard the voice of their supplication and delivered them from their fears and watered the deserts in their life. This is the kind of experience that man can get no glory out of. She herself can testify that God has the power to show you that he's God. Whether it was sparing your child's life in the womb or healing your body of cancer when the doctor said there was no hope. A person who worships money has a hunger that will never be satisfied. For we all know that money is the root of all evil and many a brother has been slain for the love of money. The more money you have the more money you want just like a vampires thirst for blood. Money can make you forget where you came from, just as money causes some people to lose their religion and not only walk away from God but their family as well. Money opens a gambit of things and stirs the demons within. Money will never give you peace without the love of Jesus Christ and the Power of the Holy Ghost. You see the love of money is a staircase leading straight to hell as you marvel at the exotics along the way. The more money the greater the expenses and after you've eaten the best foods, indulged the finest chocolates, taken your milk baths, traveled from coast to coast, kept your youth with face lifts, medicated yourself just to sleep, smoked your imported cigars, dranked from the finest wales, paid for pleasure, stomached everyone and everything around you the demons of your mind never go away. In this corridor are the sorrows of your childhood, the abuse or neglect of a parent, down that corridor are the memories of molestation, divorce, the feeling of worthlessness, trapped within that corridor is the sorrow of a child you aborted, locked behind that corridor are your alter egos, back behind that corridor is the place were you locked up the memories of all your soul-ties. Are you tormented by demonic voices because you were the molester, murderer, rapist, missing parent, adulteress, whoremonger or abuser as you're taunted by the memories and the pain of why, why, why? As you awake and repeat yet another day of this vicious cycle, which has become the mulberry bush of your life? How could you have forgotten your cries to God, when you were down and out at the lowest point of your life, battling the spirit of suicide, homeless and strung out with nowhere to turn? Yet you called out to God with the voice of death and God stepped in by faith and blessed you but as soon as the riches poured in the more you forgot about God. Now God has become just a faint memory in your mind slowly being washed away by the rivers of greed and wantonness. And even though you now drive a luxury car which draws the attention that you've desired all your life it still didn't deliver you from a lack of self-esteem and as quiet as it's kept it's not you they like; it's the dollar sign your car represents. Oh and by the way if you never had friends and now you're swarming with them it's not you they're attracted to but how you represent opportunity. She just trying to help somebody by saying beware of cunning spirits because they'll bleed you until you're bone dry and then it's on to the next. Are you guilty of trying to keep up with everybody else? She's referring to those of you who bought that lavish house that you know you couldn't afford. A vacation is out the question because you need overtime on every paycheck and your ends still don't meet. God forbid sickness calls and if thats not enough weight for you to carry let me add this. You're one day away from divorce and a paycheck away from losing the house and car that has enslaved you. Talk about putting a strain on your marriage; money will seperate a marriage quicker than adultery will just take a poll and you'll be surprised to see how many marriages were destroyed due to lack money or misuse of money. So ask yourself. What do I love? Your answer will reflect your worship. You'll be surprised at the number of people who are guilty of worshiping money which is the God of their life at the risk of loosen their soul. It's time to tell Satan loose me and let me go. You see the unsaved me use to be a brawler when she was of the world but in Gods world the saved me learned how to hold her peace forwarding all issues to heaven by faith because the church has become a place of foolery and usury. Allow her to elaborate. As the saved me navigates through the church she suffered some grave pain. You see when she was unsaved and of the world if someone stepped on her toes she retaliated. But in Gods world the saved me learned to suffer right for wrong by holding my peace and letting the Lord fight my battles. (Help me Lord) In the world anything and everything goes. But in Gods world you must turn the other cheek. (Help me Lord) In the world you fight, curse, cut, light them up "she not talking about that skunk, cush or purple haze you smoke that got your lips blue/black" and so many other ungodly things. In Gods world you watch fast and pray. In the world you drink, smoke, lay-up, and party. In Gods world you praise, worship and keep the faith. In the world you have no rules or regard for others because you're manipulative and deceitful. In Gods world you ask for forgiveness as you forgive your fellow brethren. In the world there are no boundaries or limitations. In the world you have the Ten Commandments; In the world people are ruthless and without control. In Gods world there are rules; In the world you make your own rules. In Gods world you trust and obey the Word of God. She can speak only for herself; if it wasn't for Gods mercy and grace she would've been dead and tossed into the fires of hell ever so many years ago. As she lived like a heathen, played russian roulette in bed, drove drunk, was high off prescription pills and choked out by the hands of a man on several occasions what a sick pleasure. Need she say more concerning the depth of her wickedness or for those of you holier than thou's ungodliness? Or how about she just soften the blow all together and just say sins. And that's just what they're doing to the Bible as they change the Word of God by replacing the words with easy to stomach words or they take things out totally and that's why so many people are bound and ignorant concerning the Word of God. But by God's grace and favor she arose victorious through obedience and the receiving of the Holy Ghost. While she's at it let her say this. Some people are sovereignly selected by God to go through but remember whatever God does in your life proves his case for your life and everything that happens to you happens for you because there's one thing she learned for sure haters come with miracles. This is a Word to the Wise your problems are far beyond family, money, and self but there is hope and you can rejoice in knowing that God never waste pain and all your tears are bottled. That's why as a Child of God it's very important to have a personal relationship with God and know your craft. It's a shame to say if the Bible could talk it would tell on those of you who only open it on Sunday. Let her help somebody. You can't survive off natural food only you need spiritual food as well. Let's shift gears for a moment. Has anyone ever been blindsided? Even though the saved her character was assassinated by the self-righteous God left her with an even greater testimony. Walk with the saved me as she shares her personal experience of spiritual rape. You see the saved her was openly persecuted for her book which told her life's story. The saved me couldn't understand how some people could be so angry and bitter concerning another person's deliverance. I'm telling you the saved me was baffled at how some of the people in the church only saw the whoredoms. She couldn't for the life of her understand how her life story was used against her. Instead of them rejoicing with her some of them became a terror by spewing discord and trying to tarnish the work of God in her saved life. You know it's funny now that she thinks about it. When she would pass by some of them it was as if they'd smelt a dirty diaper and she know she smelt good because she wore Angel. Whenever the saved her was in the presence of unsaved people it was as if they saw a blossoming rose with the fragrance of hope for themselves. Can someone please tell me what's wrong with this picture? Her Pastor was established with his own charter and 501c.3 when God spoke to him in his office. "Travel help churches" Not long after he acted out of obedience and without fear of the unknown he stepped into the deep water. He retired and she resigned as they locked arms and followed the spiritual bread crumbs along the way. Let her give you some history about herself you see her testimony is all over the world and the Man and Woman of God were fully aware and had received a signed copy because Elder and her had traveled back and forth frequently the year prior. They even brought a mentor during one of their visits because the person hadn't been there in over twenty-five years. You see her husband was a student in college when God saved him. Shortly after he was ordained he returned to his home where he Pastored his first Church as he continued to preach the gospel. She's reminded of how excited the Woman of God was as she stated "you have a beautiful spirit, a pure spirit, you truly love God and you're on fire for the Lord." As she continued sweet lady of whom God has delivered from much: this town is known as the preacher's grave yard and there's a spirit of jealously here. Whatever you do sweet lady don't allow anyone to steal your praise. As the Woman of God would reach out to embrace her while saying "pray for me" accompanied with a hug and a kiss. Yet she noticed how the Woman of God would pick at her testimony. She was appalled to witness this Woman of God bouncing around the altar as she began to tell a story of how she went after her very own sister with intent to harm her and boy did she express it. As she walked the pulpit and continued to say "us women down here don't play about our husbands we'll cut you and still be saved." My mouth flew open so wide; I had to close it with my hand. She couldn't believe what she had just witnessed in the House of God and on top of that this was suppose to be a holiness church. There were other times when she witnessed the first lady verbally assaulting members by calling them stupid across the pulpit. Well she had her open embarrassment when she was forced to join the choir in which the first lady was the only one who could shake your hand as a form of entry into her choir but when the time came for the first lady to shake her hand she left her standing with her hand out. Why not? She might as well tell it all. She'd never seen a Woman of God refuse to pray for someone who was in despair. That was hard for her to spiritually digest especially when she saw the level of commitment and loyalty from the member who was reject by her first lady and denied prayer. Have you experienced this? Have you ever asked your pastor to pray for you and instead of them beginning to pray for you the pastor say's I'll be praying or maybe the pastor said God already knows? Only you can answer that question. This member gave loyalty a new definition. I can understand wanting to be a blessing to the Man of God and Woman of God but not to the extent of pawning your wedding ring. I'm telling you that member was loyal but she finally got her deliverance as she was freed from her bondage with that ministry. Where do you draw the line? Either you have the money for the Pastor's church anniversary or you don't because you can't draw blood from a turnip. This church counted chickens so that the Man of God would know the exact amount of money to be collected from the dinners sold after sunday service. I'm reminded of a Elder who was preaching a homecoming service and the daughter of the Pastor of that church saw her and ran up to her with joy while she was talking with another First Lady. She was so excited unbeknown to us as she broke in between us and reached out to get her attention. Sister you wrote a book? She turned and smiled yes ma'am. As she continued to talk without taking a breathe. I was on the computer looking up Elder's web site and you popped up. I bought your book. Wow, wow I want to write a book. I'm amazed. How did you do it sister? Not long after that day things changed she noticed that every time she went to church they would preach on whoredoms in one fashion or another. It wasn't that she was offended; I guess she felt like if you were going to preach on whoredoms you should preach it right that it might save a soul. Can you imagine the humiliation she suffered while sitting in service as the pastor begins to say "this is for all you old men who marry a younger woman one day your plumbing will stop working, yeah some of us brothers know all too well don't we?" As some of the men began to laugh as they co-signed his statement as he continued on to say "she's going to become a cougar and leave you for a younger man" I'm telling you this Man of God threw off on the Elder every chance he got. How degraded she felt when the Pastor stated across the pulpit to his congregation. "How are yawl so called saved women going to let a whore have more faith than you? and how yawl saved women going to let a whore take a Man of God that belongs to you?" She stood up and began to shout and put the very statement that Satan meant for her hurt under her feet with a Shabach! When they got home her husband apologized to her as he expressed his own hurt. The enemy was using the Man of God and Woman of God to attack the saved her. She couldn't believe how they began to preach on her by using her testimony and her deliverance against her. She's reminded of how the Woman of God questioned the terror in the night across the pulpit during a choir meeting. As the Woman of God say's to the choir has any of you ever heard about things that ride you while you sleep or something jumping on you while you sleep? You see the saved her describes in her life testament something that rides you while you sleep. It's so strong and terrifying you can hear it coming but you can't open your eyes or wake yourself up as you feel the evil and fear overtakes you. Even though you scream and fight the evil spirit is so powerful and paralyzing as it pins you down and tries to enter your mouth or choke you. This demonic spirit can cause you to become afraid to sleep and no this is not the same as the so called witch riding your back. She thinks of how the first lady made a mockery of her because of the first lady own disbelief. Oh but look at God! You see the first lady went as far as to ask by show of hands "is there anyone who has ever heard or experienced this? The saved her didn't say a word because she knew God had her back and slowly but surely the hands of several choir members began to go up in the air. Well, what is it the Woman of God asked? Then she quickly abandoned the subject but not before there was a loud unidentified thump in the sanctuary. The noise was so loud that everyone began to try to find the cause of the mysterious sound when clearly there was nothing standing, hanging or sitting in the area in which the sound came from. Talk about strange; that area just happened to be where the black piano sat. The saved her is here to tell you country style; folk better stop playing with God and his anointed. You wouldn't believe the number of members and not just women that came to the saved her and told her that after reading her life testament or hearing her testify they were able to become freed from hidden sins and secrets that they were ashamed to speak of in times past as some would say the Woman of God tells us not to testify on certain things. This is for all of you that say church hurt doesn't exist because if that's not enough church abuse she just described lets talk about how the Man of God would attack her testimonies as well. She's telling you the devil was busy within those church walls as he used that Man of God and Woman of God to try and suffocate the Jesus within her. If this is your experience and you've been told that church hurt isn't real you better run, run, run. The saved her was shocked when the Man of God criticized her for quoting chapters out the Bible as she sometimes do when she testify. You see she prayed a prayer and God honored it. She prayed to God asking God to allow her mind to become a mental rolodex of the Word of God that she may be able to pull it up via any situation or circumstance. The saved her couldn't understand why the Man of God would dig out from under the Word of God and attack her testimony. Man of God, Woman of God and all of you that are a part of their posse if you're reading, judging and criticizing this book. Then tell me were you calling her a devil when you said across the pulpit after she'd testified in which she quoted Psalms 27 that the devil know the Word of God to? Let her clarify something. She fears no man and that includes woman because if the truth be told some of you are going to find yourself in a burning hell behind all the cover up pertaining to this Man of God and Woman of God. You can't say that you weren't warned remember God needs no one but he uses man and woman so take heed. This is a Word to the Wise God is the only one you should fear because as long as you tuck tail and run behind a man the further away you'll get from God. People of God right is right and wrong is wrong. So ask yourself. How can the Man of God or Woman of God speak on your behalf concerning your entry into Heaven if they're in hell? Did you know that the private conversations between the pastor and a member should never come across the pulpit? The pulpit should never be used to intentionally assassinate Gods people. How can you justify the Man of God sitting in the pulpit talking about how raggedy a members house is when his house is paid off because of their offerings? Let me be very clear Men of God and Women of God should be blessed but when a Man of God or Woman of God begins to humiliate their congregation thats not of God. The pulpit should be used to preach the Word of God not to attack the People of God. Moving right along can somebody tell me why is a whore so hated by some people in the church arena? Will you be found guilty of this hatred at your time of judgment?

Everyone knows the church is full of x-pimps, x-prostitutes, x-crackheads, x-dope feens, x-alcholics, x-drunkards, x-gamblers, x-whoremongers, x-adulterers and x-homosexual. Has it ever dawned on you that your Pastor and First Lady were delivered from some of the very same things that you can't forgive others for yet you love their dirty____ (Thank God for deliverance) She's trying her best to make it plain. Let her take this moment to give you some history about Rahab. Rahab whose name means insolence, fierceness, broad and spacious. Rahab the one time heathen harlot. Harlot meaning prostitute, whore, call girl or innkeeper. Rahab was a woman who yielded herself indiscriminately to ever man approaching her. Rahab indulged in venal wantonness, prostitution and harlotry with moral revulsion and social ostracism. Oddly enough women like Rahab are often sinned against than sinners. Whether it was molestation as a child, rape, spousal abuse or a generational curse. Man's lust for the unlawful is responsible for harlotry. God warns us of sexual sin and the prostitutes trap. Many strong men have been slain by means of a woman with a whorish spirit. For a whore is a deep ditch and a strange woman is a narrow pit, her middle is as the gates of hell, her mouth is a deep pit, as she flatter with words smoother than oil. Her lips drop as a honeycomb, her house is the way to hell, going down to the chambers of death. That's for all of you who love the pure unadulterated Word of God. Rahab was a sinful woman who God purged and grace erased her former life of shame. It was business as usual when someone came seeking Rahabs favor. This was a Godly man not a idolater and he was bent on one mission. Harlot though Rahab was she was able to discern that he was a Man of God. People of

God gifts and callings are without repentance. This man was a forerunner of Gods will and Rahab discerned that to take sides with him would be to take sides with God himself. Further in Rahabs mind know matter how faintly she understood Rahab was a believer and knew that she was being singled out from her own idolatrous people to aid the God in whom she had a growing conception of. Rahab had a deep desire to be separated from such a doomed people and identified with the People of God. You see Rahab woke up to a day no different than any other day but by night fall Rahab was faced with a deadly decision. Life or death? Knock, knock. As I could only imagine Rahab opening the door with the words, gentlemen, what's your pleasure on this fine evening? You see Rahab was a woman who was trusted and entrusted; she was the towns vault so to speak. You see Rahab held the town secrets of those such as business men, lawmen, politicians and men of the clergy. With that being said she knew that no one wanted their dirty laundry aired so to speak. Think about it. The law knocked at Rahab's door they didn't proceed to ransack her establishment by turning over beds, checking closets or shaking down her customers. They quietly and peaceably ask Rahab a question and Rahab answered and the lawmen proceeded on their way. (Now you must remember when all this transpired Rahab wasn't saved) Rahab planned his protection and escape and in doing so she received from him a promise "when we return to your country you and your family will be spared alive." As he instructed her to place the scarlet line out of the same window that they were lowered down by and speak not a word least you break the promise between us. As he continued to stress to Rahab if anyone be found outside your house their blood is on their own head. Rahab kept her word and he kept their promise. Whereby under the protection of the scarlet line Rahab and all her kindred were brought out of the house and spared alive. We cannot but admire Rahab's courage and willingness to risk her own neck. Rahab the muddy and defiled woman became the fountainhead of the river of the water of life which floweth out of the throne of God and the lamb. Rahab's name became sanctified and ennobled and is worthy of inclusion among many saints. Rahab was brought out of an accursed city and from her own sins which were as a scarlet. Rahab is a fitting illustration of another miracle of divine grace; namely the calling forth of Gods church out of a godless gentile world. Rahab became a faithful follower of the Lord. Her remarkable faith was a sanctifying faith leading her to a pure life and honorable career. The gratitude of one of the men in which she had hidden ripened into love and when grace erased her former life of shame, the Man of God made her his wife. (Talk about going from the pit to the pulpit) What a vein of gold that was in such a despised character. When the mighty change took place in Rahab's life and she was transformed from a whore into a worshipper of Jehovah. Her tribute to God's omnipotence and sure triumph over his foes reveals a spiritual insight God grants to all who believe. God restored to honor and holiness the redeemed harlot and her family. We are reminded by Rahab's change of heart and life that the blood of Jesus can make the vilest clean. For the blood of Jesus avails, whereby the worst of sinners can be saved from sin and hell. If there is anyone reading this book and you are outside the ark of safety. I want you to know that while the door of grace and mercy stands ajar, the vilest sinner can return and know what it is to be saved and safe. For Rahab is a living witness and testament of God's saving grace and she's not ashamed to say that she was once a queen of darkness but it was by faith that she's now free. By faith Rahab became one of God's heroines and is included among the harlots entering the Kingdom of God before the self-righteous. Talk about God's super-natural ability to heal, deliver and set free. And if that's not enough Rahab is the only woman besides Sarah who is designated as an example of faith in the great cloud of witnesses. What a manifestation of divine grace it is to find the one time harlot ranked along with saints like Enoch, Noah, Abraham, Joseph, Moses, and David! Man of God, Woman of God, Mothers Board, Usher and Members if Rahab stood before you in your congregation how would you treat her? Would you receive Rahab with open arms and love or would you treat Rahab the way you treated the saved me? I'm your modern day Rahab who was set free from harlotry by the Power of God and placed beside a Man of God. So this statement goes out to the hand full of you so called Men of God and Women of God who treated me like the plague now you know beyond a shadow of a doubt who you would've been in Rahab's day; by the way you've persecuted me in my day. "My God Today" As the saved her prays that you get delivered and God has mercy on your soul because Rahab just might be the gate keeper on the day your number is called and if you haven't repented for the way you tortured the saved me Rahab will be waiting for you with Holy Ghost deuces (As China K. would say.) "My, my, my" People of God that's why it's so important that no matter what situation life throws your way you must learn to say

Hallelujah anyhow. You know God has his choices. Let's talk about Hosea. Hosea was known as the Prophet of a sorrowful heart. The Word of the Lord said to Hosea, go and take unto thee a wife of whoredoms and children of whoredoms. So he went and took Gomer the woman infamous for her harlotry. Gomer means completion: which is the filling up of the measure of idolatry or ripeness of consummate wickedness. Her name was indicative of the wholesale, adultery and idolatry of the kingdom she represented. Gomer was a woman of sensual pleasure and became the wife of Hosea the godly prophet. Which symbolized God's grace as she was plucked from the hand of Satan but the evil taint was in Gomer's veins and having inherited immoral tendencies they manifested themselves again. (Gomer is a prime example of a generation curse) Thus as the unfaithful wife of the Prophet, Gomer went deeper into sin left Hosea and became the slave of one of her paramours. Commanded by God Hosea obeyed God and loved a woman who's yet an adulteress. Hosea thus out of his anguish rises to a deeper understanding of the forgiving love of God. As he bought Gomer back for fifteen pieces of silver, a homer of barley and a half homer of barley. Hosea must have been some kind of man to obtain a wife of whoredoms in the first place. As he showed no resentment when told to buy her back after she had returned to her old lovers. (This is a true example of obedience to the will of God) If Hosea's love enabled him to take back his poor, misguided, repentant wife, how much more will the love of God receive us graciously and love us freely? The love of Hosea for his wayward wife was not destroyed by her betrayal and unfaithfulness. Yet out of all this process of pain there came full confidence in God for the ultimate victory. As Hosea say's to Gomer thou shalt abide for me many days, thou shalt not play the harlot; and thou shalt not be for another man; so will I also be for thee. Through Hosea and Gomer's trial we see the forgiveness of sin, the power of love, faith and the fullness of joy. As a wife of whoredoms regarded as an adulteress Gomer became a symbol of her people as the wife of Hosea the Godly Prophet. Who symbolized God's grace in taking out of a world which had whorishly departed. Gomer was sanctified by communion with the prophet amid much personal anguish: Hosea came to see in his own suffering a reflection of what the sorrow of God must be when his church proves utterly unfaithful through self-righteousness and the inability to love. How marvelous is our Lord and Savior Jesus Christ whom unites to himself the unholy to make holy. What a lesson learned from a broken heart. Anguish quickens apprehension; iniquity inspires moral indignation, suffering begat sympathy and the divine character sanctifies human conduct. So the Prophet Hosea was not only Gods messenger of grace his story is a perfect illustration of Gods unfathomable love. You see Hosea didn't disregard Gods request to go and take Gomer as his wife instead Hosea obeyed God. Which reminds her of her obedience to the voice of God you see she has several testimonies concerning obeying God. One day she was headed to work as she approached the railroad tracks a voice said plant a two thousand dollar seed and I'll see that the education is paid in full. She smiled and repeated out loud what she had just heard as she continued on to work. When she returned home later that evening she told the Man of God about her experience and his exact words were "sweetheart I'll never get in the way of what God tells you to do" So she planted the two thousand dollar seed without thought. Now it's not like she's rich two thousand dollars is two thousand dollars. She was thinking that God was referring to her oldest child because at the time he was a sophomore in college, one was a junior in high school and another was a sophomore in high school. To make a long story short one day her husband was taking her to her relief point and as they sat her phone rang. Hello. Hello, may I speak to so and so. She responded I'm their provider and they aren't with me at this present time. Ok, well provider this is a College and I'm calling because they have been accepted into our program. She quickly cut in ma'am how much is this going to cost me? Provider it's all been paid in full for them. She replied ma'am I have one in college so I know it's going to cost me something. She responded provider not only is their education paid in full they will get paid every Friday and when they complete all their courses and receive their diploma, they will receive a lump sum of money as she continued on to say provider all we need is for them to be at the downtown greyhound station Tuesday morning at 8:00 am which meant I had only four days to get them prepared. Don't tell me what obedience to God and faith in God won't do. Now let me share with you one of her husband's personal experiences from his mouth to her hand as you read along. One of his biggest concerns when he went before God pertaining to marrying her was God can I trust her. He knew the unsaved her was controlling of men because he witnessed it with his own eyes and ears but to his surprise the unsaved her had a continual interest in God and a pure desire to learn more about God.

So he felt obligated to share the Word of God with her as he invited her to a Bible study. He was shocked to find out how intelligent she was as he quickly realized that he had fallen in love with her with a full understanding that she was no ordinary woman. You see she was a woman with a dark past to say the least and the fear of being with this type of woman could only be conquered by keeping his faith in God. He'd never seen a woman with so many gifts before she's a prophetess, she's a dreamer of dreams, she's a woman of vision, she's a woman of strong faith, she's very discerning and if thats not enough she can qoute entire chapter's out the Bible as if she's reading straight from the pages of the Bible. The things that she's spoken have come to pass one-hundred percent. He has actually experienced this woman hear the voice of God which became evident because she writes down all her dreams, visions and spoken words given to her by God. And sure enough they come to pass. If he begin to tell you his story it would be a book inside a book so he'll keep it simple. This woman has continued to come forward and he's continued to see her grow and to his surprise she has become a wonderful Woman of God. She has proven her ability to separate the Pastor from the husband, the church from her private life and the separation between mother, children, family and friends. His only regret is the experiences she's had since she's left her world and entered into his world with total surrenderance. He's witnessed her suffer from the hands of the church and he's seen her suffer from not living the lifestyle that she's accustomed to living. He is in total shock at how the church has treated this woman. He never would've imagined or believed the cruelty, anger, hatred and unwelcomed vibe she experienced from the holiness church. This woman has witnessed a Preacher steal his offering and not just one time. She has been hit on by a Pastor that he introduced to her as his friend. Just as he himself witnessed Preachers hit on her, talk about her, turn their noses up at her, along with their wives and even look at him differently. He's had Preachers look pass him to try and handle his wife but truth be told if it wasn't for God none of us could handle her. It's only because he's been ordained to be her husband and God has placed a special love in her heart for him because only God can keep this woman. He doesn't have fame, fortune or position; he's just a humble Man of God seeking to do the will of God with this Woman of God. Many doors have closed in his face because of the hatred towards his wife's life testament but for every door that closes God's going to open seven. He knows that there are other Men of God and Women of God that have suffered like them and one day they'll meet as he waits for his opportunity to shine in the Kingdom of God even though sometimes it seems as though they stand alone. (Bless you Man of God) Why do you categorized sin? And why is your forgiveness limited to the level of sin committed? I read that sin is sin and love covers a multitude of sins. (Preach!) Let's talk about a nameless biblical woman. Sinners were treated with sanctimonious contempt just as she was treated except she's saved and was being judge by her past sins which were under the blood of Jesus which makes anyone of you who went under the blood a blood washed demon. While Jesus was sitting instructing the people some religious leaders brought in a woman. These were men with corrupt hearts whose zeal against the sins of others was only a cloak to cover their own vileness having eyes full of adultery themselves as they gazed at the naked woman who was taken in the act of adultery. How partial the accusers were! They brought the woman who was taken in the act of adultery but where was the man the chief offender? Why wasn't he brought? Was it because he was one of them? (Things that make you say hmmm) Instead the woman had to bare the severity of the offense. (Thank God divine justice is without partiality) Could anything have been more cruel or harsh? This conduct showed on the religious leader's part to be a cold, hard, cynicism, a graceless, pitiless, barbarous brutality of one's heart and conscience. Because of the humiliation the saved her suffered from religious leaders she understood the shame of the nameless biblical woman who was taken in the act of adultery. Her life testament was paraded around cruelly among leadership as several members from surrounding churches were asked in secret to read her testimony and then share their opinion. And sure enough someone let the cat out the bag. There's one thing she can attest to God didn't let anything sneak up on her no matter how painful. There's always a bumble bee in the mist just as the church is full of busy bodies. (The saved her just had to go on and say that maybe it will help somebody) Allow her to give you a bit of advice if you'll receive it. Be slow to condemn another persons sin; without condemning every sin in your own life. Jesus never excused sin in those who came his way; Jesus was ever tender and gracious in his treatment of them. So we as the people of God should declare to every sinner God's forgiveness. Don't allow that cunning old serpent satan to allow you to become as the self-righteous with no expression of forgiveness or peace. Preach on if you will. This is a Word to the Wise don't allow adultery which takes its place in the front ranks as the works of the flesh manifested of wickedness to become your stumbling block. If anyone has had their head on a chopping block by some of the church folk you have to recognize that they have a religious-spirit and are in need of prayer and deliverance. Whether the spirit is seating in the low seat clear on up to the high seat. The only thing you need to remember is Hallelujah anyhow. (That felt good to my sanctified soul) My, my, my moving right along. You may ask yourself why did Jesus look down? What did Jesus right on the ground? But it was what Jesus said. He that is without sin among you let him cast the first stone. Now facing her Jesus asked. Where are thine accusers? Have no man condemned thee? The woman simply answered. No man, Lord. It was at that defining moment that the woman received her deliverance as she recognized that Jesus was the only one who had the right to pass judgment on her. As she stood in silence Jesus said to the woman go and sin no more. This is a Word to the Wise if you choose to live a Godly life you'll be persecuted so put your feelings in your pocket and except that with every level there's a new devil. Looking back she couldn't quite understand the feelings the person she looked up to had toward the church but surely now after her own personal experience she can see exactly what happened to that person. You see she herself now know the pains of church hurt because she herself has suffered the abuse of the self-righteous toward her and this is the best way she know how to describe what this type of pain feels like "it feels like you've been split to the white meat." You see the person she looked up to was married to a saved person who was much older than they were as the saved person established them on another level in their christian walk. You see they were worldly being yet made an honest person through marriage. Yet unable to separate and fully submit to being born again they remained in bondage as they were bound by the generational curses of their blood line. The torment of the self-righteous and the separation from their family was to grave for them to bare. In fact if they hadn't returned to them which were their first love it would have been their grave. So they returned to their wicked ways as they was unable to get the victory over the old woman. The abuse that they suffered from the self-righteous within the church house had become as poison running through their veins which caused them to become bitter and to turn away from God. She's not saying by any means that they don't believe that there's a God. In her heart of hearts she know that they believe in God but somewhere in between they got lost. You see the love they have for their family ultimately became the stumbling block of their life. So many people have fallen victim to this subtle matter concerning the heart but I urge you to reevaluate your choice because God is a jealous God. And if you're honest with yourself you know that the very ones you chose over God will leave you in the cold before they will ever offer you the warmth of their home. In their words "God bless the child that's got his own" until they spend their last penny gambling and need you to keep their lights on. (Just some food for thought it wasn't meant to choke you) This is something the saved her know all too well. As she's reminded of how painful her trial of seperation was. There're no words to explain or express the feeling except to say it feels as though your heart is being ripped out of your chest. The pain of separation is a tearing so grave it's breath taking almost as if the life is being sucked straight out of you. It feels as if death has hit you and this is something that you can never prepare for. She's telling you it wasn't easy it took every bit of her faith; because anything and everything the enemy could find to cause her to stumble he threw her way. But she was determined to live a sanctified life her mind was made up and it was a settled matter. She was going to keep her personal relationship with God as well as her peace and sanity because it was one thing she knew for sure whatever she had to go through was worth her sobriety, virtue and sound mind. You see she knew God had plucked her straight from the pit of hell and she's been running, running, running ever since and through the Power of the Holy Ghost she continually arises victorious. Not only did God mend her broken heart those people who use to call and torment her by saying that she had gone crazy in religion had finally gained a new found respect and a greater understanding of her commitment to God. Brace yourself; here comes the first triple loop of the roller coaster ride of her life. She thought that she had experienced the greatest test of her Christian walk which was seperation but little did she know there was a greater test lying ahead. She didn't know whether to inhale or exhale because the roller coaster of her life was so intense. Let's talk about those southern most states. These are the states with doors of great secrets amid such a religious people. Those of whom act holier than thou as if their sinless and guiltless. Let's shine the light on the girls who delivered their father's, uncles, brothers, cousin or pastor baby. If grass could talk it would tell you how many babies that are buried within the backyards of many by way of something as simple as a coat hanger or a concoction. (Sounds like murder to me but who am I to say) And then you have the nerve to get angry with God after the death of your child. As you sob nearly to death but where were the tears for the two you aborted. Did you ever stop to wonder how God felt after you murdered one of his precious little angels that was developing within your womb. What about the shame of an unwed child becoming pregnant and being sent away until after the birth of the child? As she was forced to give her baby to one of her family members who couldn't bare children and told never to speak of it. As the family member raises the child and they grow up as cousins only to find out later that your cousin is really your mother. We can't leave out all you woman who sit on the front row of the church house and cradle the Pastors child even though he's married and you know sister so and so is rocking his baby to. It amazes me the depths of betrayal people use just to cover sin and save face before people with total disregard toward the Commandments of God. (Such as the world) That might have been a hard read but somebody got their deliverance as they read their truth. She think on how she was given a last name that didn't belong to her just so her parent could avoid the criticism and cover up the fact that the siblings had different fathers. I guess they never stopped to think about the effect that decision would have on the childs life. Talk about things done in the dark coming to light. At the age of eleven through a sudden divorce she was introduced to her birth father yet the only memory she has is at the age of eleven she became fatherless. She doesn't have a story of being daddy's little girl or princess. The only story she has to tell is that her father was stolen from her all because of people who would rather cover up sin then to forgive. As a result she became the victim even though she was the innocent one caught in a tangled web of deceit weaving with secrets. Do you know how devastating this was in her life? Talk about a game changer. Imagine a man thinking the child is his and out of know where the child falls gravely ill and the father is willing to give an organ only to find out that he's not a match. Let her clarify something. She loves the person that she looked up to and she places no blame on them. She learned a lot of things from them and everything that she picked up wasn't bad. You see for the better part of her life which was the first eleven years she learned how to cook, clean and serve a man. She learned how to properly pronounciate, she learned etiquette and above all she learned how to be a strong woman when faced with adversity. Her mentor is a loving person; they will give you the shoes off their feet, clothes off their back and as close to their last dime as they could give and thats the God's truth. She's come to learn that they are trapped in the corridors of their mind drowning in past memories of their trespasses and those who have trespassed against them. She solicit all prayer warriors to go warring against the demonic forces in her mentors life that they may receive true deliverance and total healing before that great day. (I decree and declare that it is so in the mighty name of Jesus.) I understand how they lost their way as they became dazed, confused, without direction, void of love, incapable of loving and receiving love as their heart became hardened toward man. You see when some people grow up without the love of their mother it becomes almost impossible for them to fully love. If a child is left behind or given up for adoption there's a feeling of being unwanted within them which is as a unanswerable why? These feelings generally follow them throughout their life and in some cases it causes drug abuse, depression and in more severe cases suicide. My mentor became consumed with grief and returned to their comfort place where they were accepted without judgment and here's the punch line. The enemy used the self-righteous to destroy her mentor spiritually which was the same tactic that the enemy used on her but God. Remember you're on my roller coaster so I'm giving you a heads up there's a tunnel up ahead followed by a winding turn. People of God how could you become one who causes another to stumble? Did you know that makes you an enemy to the cross? People of God take heed time is winding up and it's now time to do some serious soul searching. This question is directed to all Preachers. Are you guilty of pernicious preaching? Pernicious means to have a harmful, damaging, evil, wicked, poisonous and corrupting effect in a gradual or subtle way. This kinda reminds me of being in an abusive relationship with a man who blacks your eye and then say's I'm sorry I won't hit you again, so he breaks your arm the next time. You see there are so many lost souls due to false prophets who privily shall bring in damnable heresies and many shall follow their pernicious ways; by reason of whom the way of truth shall be evil spoken of and through covetousness shall they with feigned words make merchandise of you. For if God spared not the angels that sinned but cast them down to hell and spared not the old world but saved Noah and yet turned the cities of Sodom and Gomorrah into ashes. The Lord knoweth how to deliver the Godly out of temptations and to reserve the unjust unto the day of judgment to be punished. This is a Word to the Wise you better get your life right! People of God that's why it's extremely important that you have a personal relationship with God so as not to fall into the trap of being a personality worshipper or bound within a church because of a pernicious Man of God and or Woman of God. People of God you must study the Word of God that you don't become one who's lead astray through false doctrine's and traditions of men. (There's a hidden nugget before your very eyes to all the seer's) The book of Ezekiel is a prime example of how God almighty sits high and looks low. Stay with me now I'm going somewhere! (Ezekiel 34:2-20) Son of man, prophesy against the shepherds of Israel, prophesy, and say unto them, Thus saith the Lord God unto the shepherds; Woe be to the shepherds that do feed themselves! should not the shepherds feed the flocks? Ye eat the fat, (Glutton) and ye clothe you with the wool, (rhinestone's head to toe) ye kill them that are fed: but ye feed not the flock. The diseased have ye not strengthened, neither have ye healed that which was sick, neither have ye bound up that which was broken, neither have ye brought again that which was driven away, neither have ye sought that which was lost; but with force and with cruelty have ye ruled them. And they were scattered, because there is no shepard: and they became meat to all the beasts of the field, when they were scattered. (No shepherd of the ministry searched or sault after them yet you shepherds fed yourselves as a Glutton) Therefore, ye shepherds, hear the word of the Lord; As I live, saith the Lord God, surely because my flock became a prey, and my flock became meat to every beast of the field, because there was no shepherd, neither did my shepherds search for my flock, but the shepherds fed

138

themselves, and fed not my flock; Therefore, O ye shepherds, hear the word of the Lord; Thus saith the Lord God; Behold, I am against the shepherds; and I will require my flock at their hand, and cause them to cease from feeding the flock; neither shall the shephards feed themselves any more; for I will deliver my flock from their mouth, that they may not be meat for them. Sounds like God mean business concerning you perinicious Shephards "I will destroy the fat glutton and the strong; I will feed them judgment, I will require my flock at their hand that they may not be meat for them." The saved her is scared for you because God has a way of showing you that's he is God Almighty when your title, church and life style goes to your head. For the very same people that you perniciously preach on are the very same one's you may need to stand you up, wash you up and push you around. She just saying you might be tax exempt but none of us are exempt from the Word of God. She's just saying she's determined to win this race so she's very careful not to anger God, kill anyone spiritually or become someone's stumbling block because everyone is not strong enough to hold on to their Jesus after the Men of God and Women of God have assassinated their character as other Men of God and Women of God stood idly by with no rebuke. She remembers the very day the Lord spoke to her and said "get my Word and tell my story." She will not apologize for her life testament and yes she may repeat somethings several times throughout this roller coaster ride of the highs and lows of her lonesome road as she gives a Word to the Wise along the way. The unsaved her lived a very racy life but it's a true testament to the delivering Power of God. When you Men of God and Women of God got together and chewed the fat concerning her testimony did anyone of you ever stop to think about her love ones? Has it dawned on anyone of you that some of her love ones had no idea the life she lived? Did you Men of God and Women of God who turned your backs on her ever consider the threats she recieved? Did you Men of God and Women of God know that you were spitting on a work of God as your juicy mouths gossiped to one another while you read the pages of her life's testament? This is to the Man of God that said she should rewrite her life testament. "Man of God there's only one regret she has concerning her testimony and that's the editing" but yet and still she pat herself on the back just as King David encouraged himself. But while we at it let her share this intimate detail with you. Someone who at the time was only seventeen years old asked her for a copy of her testament. "Are you sure you want to know all about her life? They replied. "Yes ma'am." Well I'm not sure you're mature enough. "I'm almost grown they replied." So a signed copy with a special heart felt message was given to them. When I tell you it wasn't twenty-four hours later and the person was standing at her door crying with their arms out to hug her. The saved her said to them "are you alright?" She replied. "Already I've cried, laughed and got mad reading your life testament." As she stood in amazement saying "man I can't put it down and by the way I know who initials those are." This person didn't beat up on the saved her, they didn't tell her that they were ashamed of her, they didn't say they were embarrassed and they didn't turn their back on the saved her like you grown so called saved Men of God and Women of God did. As if you all were born Holy Ghost filled without sin or need of repentance. Don't duck and don't get mad at the truth. You know exactly who you are but you know what the good news is? If you're reading a Word to the Wise you still have a chance to repent unlike some of the other ones who died with bitterness in their hearts toward the saved her. Instead of rewarding the saved her with church hurt like you self- righteous did they showed her love and even said they were sorry for the things that she had gone through in her life. Can I say something? Yes. "You were no joke and now I know why your people didn't bother you but yet and still you gave them money whenever they were in a bind and you lived your life as if none of those things ever happened to you, you are some kind of woman." Well my mentor always told me it's nice to be nice you see it wasn't so much that she was thinking of them but it was their children she always had a concern for. Can you imagine the weight behind her exposing her life? Have you thought about the others who had no idea of what their parent did to her? Has anyone stopped to think about the pain her mentor most have felt? No. You Men of God and Women of God never stopped to think about any of those things yet you say you're holiness personified but your behavior shows you as Satan's liaison as you poured salt on a Child of God. The saved her is telling you some of the Men of God and Women of God persecuted me beyond words "talk about church hurt!" At first she didn't know how to react to such a traumatic experience. She remember her breaking point as she cried out uncontrollably. God please, she said; don't let them suck the life out of me. As her tears were blinding to her sight "I love you God" she repeated countless times. Please help me God, help me please. As she cried out to God from a spiritually broken heart. Right there she had to take a deep breathe because it was as if she was being spiritually gang raped by the Men of God and Women of God of that organization. As they ganged up and verbally assassinated the saved her. Yes! This Woman of God was being attacked because of her unsaved life in which God had delivered her out of. Help me Lord. (As I ask you Heavenly Father to hold on to me) You see she came from the street and God had gutted her. She was now a new creature in Christ so when she had this experience in the church house it completely knocked the wind out of her and I do mean literally. She could hear the faint voice of her husband the Man of God saying; this is a trick of the enemy it's not the church that has hurt you as he wiped her tears away while saying "Satan will use whom ever will yield their spirit to him and in your case it just happened to be Men of God and Women of God." Satan wants you to have a bad understanding but remember the words of your mentor who told you that the "church wouldn't welcome a woman with a past such as yours they told you that people were jealous of you when you were in the world but they couldn't handle you then and in Gods world they won't be abe to handle you either." As he went on to say above all you must keep your eyes on Jesus as he continued to speak straight into her spirit. This is a Word to the Wise it's easy to see evil when it's out front but the ones who use righteousness to cover their evil are the ones you never see coming. The enemy is laughing and he intended for you to fall at this stumbling block. As the Man of God continued to say "you've now reached a pivotal place in your life" you must remember the world is bold in their opposition. So Woman of God you must stand on a solid foundation and be rooted and grounded in the Word of

God. Listen to me sweetheart your mentor forewarned you by telling you that some church people are cruel. Your mentor also told you that your faith freed you and that it takes some longer to get to where you are and some never make it. This battle is not yours; let it go and put it in your next testament. As he began to pray for her as she gradually gained strength. She looked up and said Man of God you know you're right this is a job for Jesus. As she began to pray that God would have mercy on the Men of God and Women of God whom inflicted such pain on her by way of pernicious preaching. It might have taken you two minutes to read about this trial in her life but it took seven hundred and twenty hours for the total healing to take place. This was a devastating blow to her but she arose victorious because she can do all things through Christ that strengthens her. She would like to take this opportunity to thank her mentor for what she thought at the time was them being critical toward the church. Yet they were actually given her a tool to prepare herself for the experiences which lie ahead in her very own christian walk. She found that after dealing with the demonic forces of the world there're just as many and even greater demonic forces in the church. That's why she can't stress enough the importance of having a personal relationship with God for yourself or you'll surely stumble over the many obstacles that await your christian walk. We as the People of God must first have a clear understanding that it wasn't the church that hurt you but it was a demonic spirit operating through someone within the church that hurt you and it's of vital importance; crucial for your understanding of how to seperate the two. There are so many people wandering in a backslidden state angry and blaming God for their church hurt when God is blameless. This is a Word to the Wise it's time to revisit the source of your pain, doubt, confusion, suffering, weariness, slothfulness, abusive, abusing, addictive, argumentative, manipulative, controlling, influenced, bound corrupt mind and receive true deliverance. Did you know that if the devil can't cut you short he'll push you bye? People of God it's more to being saved and sanctified then wearing a big hat and a long skirt. You must first be renewed in the spirit of your mind, knowing that we die daily but the more Christ you put on the more the old man falls off. Remember People of God you must have a clean heart and the right spirit as a Child of God. This is a Word to the Wise don't miss your moment because of your attitude; whereby so many have stumbled and become paralyzed. People of God you must always remember that there's a continual battle between the flesh and the spirit and for all of you that didn't know slippers don't go. This is for all you slick christians. Don't get hooked on a feeling like a two minute thrill, the relaxation of a cigarette, how mellow a glass of wine is, the burn of a strong drink on your tongue and the numbness of a blow. Maybe for you it's the joy of gambling, pill popping, club hopping, lying, stealing, cheating and whore mongering or are you an idolater, agnostic or atheist? This is a Word to the Wise there is no such thing as a saved sinner so if you still practice sin you got the wrong spirit. You see the carnal mind is an enmity against God, for it is not subject to the law of God neither indeed can be so then they that are in the flesh cannot please God. People of God be not deceived according to the world and according to the prince of the power of the air. For you must understand that we are in the midst of a crooked and perverse nation where the blood thirsty hate the upright. Did you know that many Christians stager at the promises of God because of unbelief? Remember the prayer warriors who were praying for Peter's release from prison they were up all night in entercession for Peter's life but when Rhoda came running to them Peter is at the gate Peter is knock, knock, knocking at the door they called her mad do to their unbelief. Although they verbally attacked Rhoda she held firm in her belief that Peter was at the door even though she hadn't physically laid eyes on him. Rhoda recognized the voice of Peter whom she'd listen to so often expounding the Word of God and believed. Rhoda's biblical story is a great example of how some people prayers are mixed with unbelief. Tell me how can you half believe and expect a whole miracle from God? This is a Word to the Wise let God be true but every man a liar; Jesus Christ hung bleed and died on the cross for the remission of our sins! Fighting the ultimate battle defeating Satan and taken the keys to death, hell and the grave. It's either you believe or you don't. The Bible declares in (Romans 3:3-4) For what if some did not believe? Shall their unbelief make the faith of God without effect? God forbid: yea, let God be true, but every man a liar; as it is written, that thou mightest be justified in thy sayings, and mightest overcome when thou art judged. Let's talk about the unsaved her who was a loud, stubborn unlearned woman who was led astray. The unsaved her was trapped and imprisoned in her mind due to her childhood and the sexual abuse thereof. She grew to become a cold blooded, bitter, heartless woman, drowned by demonic spirits that entered into her life at a young age. The unsaved her only knew survival which brought about the root of all evil. The unsaved her was arrogant, bold, rude, angry, voicetress, unruly and cruel as she was taunted and ruled by demonic spirits. The unsaved her wore the best, drove the best and lived high on the hog. The unsaved her was subject to no man and whatever she wanted she got. The unsaved her ruled over everyone of her men as they all learned how to get in where they fit in and after all her sinful increase she would always give to others. Such as the shoes off her feet, the purse off her shoulder, pay peoples grocery bills and even pick women out during the holiday season and pay for their children's toys. The unsaved her even furnished a ladies entire house as the lady got on her bus and while paying her fare the lady began to tell her how she had no furniture and was on her way to the thrift store. The unsaved her did everything she could to help others with hopes that it would wash her sins away. You see the unsaved her was a lonely, abused, alcoholic, addicted lost soul who was helpless and seeking to be loved. The unsaved her was a woman who felt hopeless and confused as she thrived off attention which was void from that special mentor in her life. She only ever wanted to be somebody in the eyes of her mentor. Yet she never understood how her mentor put everyone above her. So she chose to mimic her mentor in hopes of gaining her mentors love and approval. So the unsaved her began studying her mentors ways and to immolate them. The unsaved her did whatever it took to hear her mentor say the one thing that she yearned for. Which were these simply little words I'm proud of you; you've turned out to be a beautiful woman, mother and daughter. Though that didn't happen her mentor did often comment on her lifestyle by saying "you took it up ten times higher than I did." You see the unsaved her always saw her mentor as a strong person who danced to the beat of their own drum. In the unsaved her eyes there was no person that could come near the greatness that she saw in her mentor. The unsaved her saw her mentor as a hero. Her mentor was a person who had suffered much as I go only by the things that they shared with me. So I sat them before me as an example of what a true person is and trust me my mentor is solid as a rock, educated, intelligent and beautiful. I saw my mentor rule every person in their life and dominate every situation without regard. My mentor is tough or should I say the spirit that lies within them. As a result of mimicking her mentor the unsaved her learned how to flatter with words, her mouth was smoother than oil, her lips dropped as a honeycomb, and her house was the way to hell going straight to the chambers of death. The unsaved me was unlearned, uncontrollable, defiant, unruly and without subjection. You see this was one of the many curses that fell upon the people in the unsaved her bloodline in which the Bible labels as an estrange people. Let me go here for a second. In the olden day people gave their children names that represented something. For instance Ichabod means the Glory of God has departed, David means beloved, Adam means of the ground, Eve means life and Sarah means princess. You must be careful what you name someone because they tend to mimic the spirit of that name. You see from birth the unsaved her was called mama. Mama is a strong matriarchal figure who rules with an iron fist. You see through the generational curses of the unsaved her bloodline she was of a matriarchal family full of strong women from her great grandmother, to her grandmother, on down to her mother straight into her. This was a breed of women who dominated. These were women who ruled their family, house and men. These were women who made their own money and decisions. Now you have a better understanding of how the unsaved her became vain, cruel, uncontrollable, materialistic, rotten, rude, superficial, heartless, cold-blooded, selfish, fake, false and void of true understanding. (The unsaved her was led by her emotions and flesh) Many women have become a product of their environment. These are women who are unable to trust and are held captive by past experiences with the inability to forgive, forget and move forward in the now. As they continually sort through the trunk of their past which blocks their future and this is due to the poisoning of their minds and the coldness of their heart. Let's talk about you men who are unqualified, without morals, ex-convicts, uneducated, addicted, whoremongers who are imprisoned in your mind, without affection, homo-sexual, molested, molester, abusive, adulterer and controlling mama's boy. Yes. Mama's boy. You can't make a sound decision you have to get your mothers approval on everything? Can you imagine how many strong men that are bound by the spirit of mama? If mama say's no, then no means no. You'll be suprised at the number of men who live their life in the shadow of pleasing their mama. It amazes me to see over grown men and women still living in mama's house waiting on dinner and secretly dating. Don't get it twisted now just because you married don't mean a thing; let's get a clear understanding the spirit of mama pores over into your marriage. I'm about to flip it right here. Men how many times in your marriage have you experienced you're wife holding out just because

148

you said or did something she didn't agree with? But as soon as you say mama I'm sorry she relinquishes control. Have you brought the bartering spirit into your marriage? I'll do this if you do that. Are you a man who stays in your man cave just to keep the peace in your home? Are you that brawling woman that the Bible speaks of? Are you taking out your past hurts on your husband/wife? Can you see how easy the abused becomes the abuser? And for God's sake stop comparing you're husband to your daddy, brother, friend, next door neighbor, your sister husband, television husband and in some cases your ex-husband. No man wants to live in comparison to another and by the way stop role playing; you must be careful what spirits you entertain in your home and marriage. Ladies please remember you didn't marry your son so stop being a mother to your husband because you can't raise a grown man. This is a Word to the Wise a christian life is an unending engagement on the battlefield but the light at the end of your lonesome road is worth all the pain. Women this is a Word to the Wise even though the lioness is the hunter she still yields to the king of the jungle. Who's the king of your world? When will you no longer serve sin? Why do you play wife? You cook, clean, pleasure, work and take care of yawl kids plus his kid that are by other women. Yes, I'm talking about those children. Yea, them right there. That's them the one's you excused him for. The one's he brought home to you that he said happened by accident and you still waiting on him to marry you but you the one he gone leave because you dried up now. You allowed him to use you up and now he's moving on to marry someone young and vibrant like you once was. Well its the truth and the truth hurts but it will set you free! Don't you know there's no such thing as common law in the sight of God? It's the world that allows commom law. So ladies why give a man your all to no avail? Where is your self-worth? Why would you allow a man to rob you of your best years and then leave you like a dried up prune? If a man has morals and truly loves you he'll make you his wife and it won't take years of dating, making babies and shacking for him to make that decision. For he who findeth a wife findeth a good thing and obtains favor with the Lord. So this is to all you women. Stop going against the Word of God by seeking a husband. You all on line, internet dating and picking up strangers in the church house as you walk around with a thirsty for love sign on your forehead. Woman be still and wait on God before you find a serial killer and never trade your self respect for a relationship and remember angry little girls grow up to be bitter old women. Question. Tell me how can you go to church sit through service, hear the Word and need prayer yet you don't go to the altar? What are you scared of? People of God tell me what's so important on that telephone that causes you to disrespect God while sitting in the House of God? I don't know which one is worse falling asleep during service or talking on the phone through the entire service and some of you Men of God and Women of God are just as guilty as you stand in the pulpit and go live while the preacher is preaching but this is the way of the world. People use their phones to document their everyday life, religous beliefs and political views before total strangers and you so holy but you co-signing abortion, homo-sexuality and many more ungodly views from certain parties and your members have now been lead in era. And you have the nerve to stand in the pupit and preach out the side of your mouth on the very things you agree on. Now try and make since out of that because me knowing you who fight everything definitely will. This is a Word to the Wise be careful of the voyeur or check your spirit to be sure you're not the voyeur because there's more then one definition. A voyeur is a person who gains sexual pleasure from watching others when they are naked or engaged in sexual activity or a person who enjoys seeing the pain or distress of others. King David was attracted by lovely women and saw a woman on the roof of a nearby house undressing and bathing the woman was Bathsheba. King David's passions were aroused as he coveted Bathsheba the wife of Uriah who was one of King David's most loyal men. Thus the triangle drama of passion, intrigue and murder begins. Bathsheba the woman whose beauty resulted in adultery, murder and the death of her newborn son. If only Bathsheba would've conducted herself like Queen Vashti when asked by her husband King Ahasuerus to display her lovely face and figure before the lustful eyes of a drunken debauchery banquet. King David and Bathsheba would've never became guilty of an egregious disgrace. (The quiet strom has just shifted gears) Let me hit this while I'm at it. This is for all you fashion models sharp on the outside but underneath you safety pinned together with your stockings tied at the knees. I haven't forgotten about you men with stains in your t-shirts and holes in your socks hidden behind those alligator shoes. Where's the substance? Are you one who disagree with everything the Pastor preach? Do you leave out during offering? Do you come after praise and worship or testimony service is over? Do you slip out during altar call? Do you go to church just to gossip and criticize? People of God did you know that sanctification starts from the inside? So if the things you indulge in lead your mind to sinful thoughts and not the cross you need to check yourself. You see now a day people go overboard taking everything to the extreme you kill my dog, I kill your cat. People of God don't be foolish we're living in a day of adversity so you must guard your gate at all times. What do you mean? Stop watching all these paranormal movies which invite fear and spirits into your house and you wonder why you sleeping with your closet light on and looking over your shoulder while going to the bathroom at night and reality television is no better because it massages your spirit and I hope you're aware that worldly music carry spirits that will take you right back to the place, year, person and child that became the result. People of God know this one thing; you don't leave God all at once you leave little by little so whatever you do don't give way to seducing spirits. It's time to wake up there's no time for spiritual immaturity you must lose the pacifier of your life whether it be the spirit of alcoholism, that dope fiend spirit, it could be the spirit of lust, gambling spirit, that foul cursing spirit, controlling angry demonic spirit, blood sucking money hungry spirit, jealous spirit, suicide demon, murder by abortion demon, backbiting, storytelling, discord sowing, division causing seed planting liar spirit, spirit of envy, malice, hatred, unforgiveness, bitterness, clamor, evil speaking, religious, self-righteous spirit all which are controlled by Satan. Now ask yourself when will I no longer serve sin? Did you know the wages of sin is death? Can you imagine the party of a life time? I mean the ultimate shebang! The smell of excrement, the taste of soot in your mouth, the visual of fire all around flickering like disco lights, the smell of burning flesh, the sound of unceasing screams, the feeling of never ending pain, over and over and over again which is the perfect ending for all of you who lived to party and satisfy you're fleshly desires. And here's the good news, you'll have all five of your best friends with you, taste, smell, hear, see and feel. This is for all of you who choose the broad way even though you heard of Jesus you yet stumbled at the pleasures of sin choosing not eternal life but total damnation. And this is what scares me the most you have no excuse because you went to church, you heard the preacher, you read the Bible yet you still stumbled because you're disobedient and you're bound by a rebellious spirit. Are you like an ostrich who buries its head in the sand? Did you know the more sins you sweep under the rug the closer the sins become to being exposed because eventually the sins will become a small mountain that can no longer be looked over. People of God it's time to get your eyes off people and stop seeking right now gratification and seek Jesus for deliverance. Let Rahab help you seeming as though she was once where you are. You see when your high has worn off you still have the same problem, pain and memories. Once the thrill is over your conscience kicks in, after the affair, comes guilt, abuse brings sorrow and your lies find you out. This is a Word to the Wise a true friend will never breech a relationship or turn your marriage to divorce; a true friend will never turn you against your spouse, become your alibi or hook you up on a blind date, double date or playdate. This is a Word to the Wise married and single don't mix. Now you're wondering why did she say that. Well allow me to shine some light in this grey area. Single people have no boundaries or limitations. Whereas married people are more family oriented, time restricted and self-contained. (Single no limits/Married restricted) Just as the saved and unsaved don't mix. (light/darkness) Now you thinking Rahab I don't agree with that. Well you tell me can you touch and agree with Satan concerning a miracle from God for you life? (If you have a answer for that I'm scared of you) The Bible states what concord hath Christ with Belial? We as the Children of God are to put a difference between holy and unholy. The Bible tells us in (2 Corinthians 6:14) Be ye not unequally yoked together with unbelievers: for what fellowship hath righteousness with unrighteousness? and what communion hath light with darkness? This next question is to all of you who are battling the spirit of alcoholism. Has that alcohol demon ever reminded you not to defile your temple before you swallow that strong drink, wine or beer? You know what I know? The spirit of alcoholism tells you you're not a alcoholic. Sure it does that demonic spirit has lead you to believe a lie even though you have a DUI and you've totaled your car not once but twice and you're still waking up in your vomit but you not a alcoholic. That demonic spirit got you telling yourself you only get drunk on the weekend so you're not a alcoholic or you're not a alcoholic because you drink after 5:00pm and you believe that lie. When has the spirit of perversion every said to you: two of the same will burn in a flame? Has the spirit of perversion ever told you that your lifestyle is against the order of God? The spirit of perversion will tell you God made you that way and you believe that lie even though the Bible gives you truth concerning the matter. Just as the world pushes all God wants us to do is love, love, love you can live how you want just love, you don't need to obey the Word of God just love,

love, love and many of you believe the lie. This is A Word to the Wise your sin is what seperates you from God. A saved person desires to live a Godly life free from sin, a unsaved person thinks it's impossible to live in this world and be free from sin. A saved person is free from bondage, a unsaved person is bound. The saved her learned through her deliverance that even though she was once bound amongst a people who she partied with, dranked with, gambled with and so many more ungodly things. When God stepped in and totally delivered her and filled her with the Holy Ghost she became an enemy to them. It's amazing how something so supernatural as God's transformation in her life caused so much hatred toward her. She was flabbergasted! You see these are those who are quick to say how blessed and highly favored they are, these were the ones who called her a sinner and said she needed to be saved. She can't even count the times she heard them call themselves a Child of God although they were in bondage as she once was. She even remember after she gave her life to Christ someone very close to her said "I better be sure I had the right God." The saved her don't fight denominations she fights sin. People of God listen up if you let bad things stop you then you won't be here for the good things. You see when she was in the world she sinned openly so she chose to expose her life through her life testament. She realize that she put herself on blast which is her cross to bare; she fully understand the scripture says for it is ashame to speak of those things but she chose to sacrifice herself in hopes that other young ladies would read and know what they too could be delivered and set free from. For she's a living testimony she's been set free and there's nothing hidden in her closet. What about yours?

People may not see in your closet but the eyes of the Lord are in every place beholding the good and the evil. Are you one who speaks peace with your mouth but mischief is in your heart? You wouldn't happen to be the one with the stone in your hand would you? I heard a Woman of God say she can't stand an adulteress woman. Well I got a question; can you stand a whoremonger son? Woman of God Rahab coming for that spirit of unforgiveness and hatred that operates through you and you know exactly who you are. My, my, my Men of God and Women of God tell me how can you pray for that adulterer who comes down on the altar when you have unforgiveness in your own heart towards adultery? Don't you know people can feel your resistance toward them? Or maybe for you it's the kindred spirit you feel which causes you to hate yourself and all the dirty secrets that follow your very own life. Let me go head on and say it! If you're a Man of God or Woman of God and you have something against adultery then you can't help this wicked, evil and adulterous generation. So you may as well hang up your gospel boots and accept your stumbling block. I'm going somewhere and if you're on this roller coaster ride of highs and lows you're going with me. Have you tried to move your church membership and the Pastor told you if you left their church you would be outside the will of God? Since when did church become a dictatorship? If the scripture say's let every man work out his own soul salvation and God has given us all free will then surely we have the right to choose where we worship. It's a devilish thing for a Man of God or Woman of God to use scare tactics to imprison a Child of God by holding them hostage against their will. Man of God or Woman of God if this is you then it changes your title from Pastor to tyrant and causes the Child of God to have a bitter spirit and a fear in their heart for man when their fear should be in our Lord and Savior Jesus Christ. (Rahab you better help somebody) Determining the will of God for someone else only shows you're out of the will of God for yourself. It's sad to say but some Pastors treat members like they belong to them instead of them belonging to God with the full understanding that their job as a Pastor is only to feed the Lords sheep not to possess them in a strange and perverse way. This is a harsh truth but somebody has to say it. You see I'm not a part of your posse; God ordained me to speak, so I'm not afraid to tell you the truth about yourself. Some pastors are preaching the same message that they've been preaching for the last twenty, thirty or forty years and haven't grown with the times in our society. Hear me now I'm not saying water down the Word of God by any means. Remember Jesus Christ is the same yesterday, today and forever but you must learn how to be skillful in presenting the Word of God to this generation. Now ask yourself; who wants chicken the same way all the time if you can go where it's served many different ways? True enough it's still chicken but it just taste better. Men of God and Women of God it's time to seek God for a fresh anointing which will enable you to snatch these lost souls out of the hand of Satan. Men of God and Women of God stop pulpit blocking and allow some of the young minister's to exercise their gift. Why are you so afraid of someone stealing your congregation if God ordained them to work with you? That type of fear is of the devil and shows your lack of faith in God. Remember everyone sitting in your congregation isn't on the same level mentally or sinfully.

Some are doctors, lawyers, business women, educated, uneducated, some have been saved their entire life so they say, some are seeking salvation, others have backslidden, some have suffered sexual abuse and in some cases it was someone in the pulpit who sexually abused them. She could go on and on but speaking from her personal experience she's found that some pastors have lost sight of the congregation and really don't know the heartbeat of the people. This question is directed to the pulpit. Is the fault found in you Man of God and Woman of God? Are you the reason your member seeks to worship elsewhere? You talk Holy but you display your unholiness as you fight and attack daily as many read your captions and cosign them all. Some of yawl need to repent because the past election drew you so far out that it left you wide open. The generation that we're in now is labeled an adulterous generation. These are those who have a different mindset, they're more perverse, wicked and much bolder. As a leader you must accept them with an open heart and not a closed mind. In the words of Nelson Mandela "If you talk to a man in a language he understands that goes to his head but If you talk to him in his language that goes to his heart." You see I know how it feels to be a survivor and a overcomer. I know what it feels like to be violated. I know all too well about cold sweats as your skin crawls yearning for a fix, I've fought the demonic voices that attacked my mind, I survived separation, I know how it feels not to be accepted, I know how it feels to step out on faith, there were times when I felt like laughing when I was crying and crying when I was laughing, you see the saved her is the real deal there's no fake and phony in her. So my question to you is have you been tried in the fire? You see Rahab was the gutter most in times past but now she's the utter most. So she encourage you to never, never, never give up, work your favor and be bold in Christ. Remember the race is not given to the swift, neither to the strong, but he that endureth to the end. Let me take this moment to shine a little light. A Man of God black balled the Elder and every door the Man of God had control over he closed. I know yawl dyeing to know what caused this to transpire but I'll just say it like this. No true Man of God will sit anywhere and watch a Man of God kill Gods people and let her make it very clear this is her summary. Moving right along and by the way there's a slow steep climb with a ferocious drop up ahead. I never saw a pastor preach a faith message close the Bible sit down and fuse a half an hour taking the Word right out of you. I was appalled. Think of it like this you've been feed a good meal and afterwards the chef sticks his finger down your throat causing you to puke it all up. Preaching is more than yelling and telling somebody that they're going to hell by trying to scare them and placing fear in their heart. Instead you as the Shepherd should offer them a solution by walking them through the Word of God and ministering to their soul while explaining to them the benefits in serving God. As the pastor you must share with them the importance of having a relationship with God and ultimately becoming a Child of God. Your responsibility as a Shepherd is to explain to them that heaven is their home and hell is a place for Satan, his demons and all who choose to follow him. Man of God/Woman of God why would you beat on a lost soul? Sometimes you have to make the Word of God sweet like candy that the person may fully understand how their disobedience and the desire to live in a sinful, cursed and worldly manner means that they choose to enjoy the pleasures of life now rather than to receive a crown of righteousness later. The Bible states that there is pleasure in sin but it's only for a season and when your season of pleasure is up there's a price to pay. So my question to you is why would you trade Heaven for Hell? How can any Shepherd rest knowing that his sheep are scattered? Inquiring minds want to know. How can a church have such a bad reputation in such a small town? It makes it hard to witness or to invite someone to church when the person you're witnessing to has something negative to say about that church in some form or fashion. Everybody's not fabricating, including Rahab. I didn't see any evil neither did I speak evil but the evil saw me and spoke about me and turned all the other First Lady's against me so now I have to bind everyone of you up! In the name of Jesus by the power of his blood I put a hook in your jaw and a cord around your tongue, I bare your jaw through with a thorn in Jesus name. I plead the blood of Jesus against you and I take authority over this foul spirit and I bind you in Jesus name. You see I'm your HUCKLEBERRY! So let me give all you who think that you're spiritual royalty you're wakeup call. The Glory of God has departed and you're not even aware. Your members have been seduced as they try to whip up some joy never stopping to see how you've destroyed families, emptied bank accounts and caused divorces. As the prophet speaks you could only hide so long and now God is about to reveal and expose. And this is to some of you ladies, your skirt tail is about to be pulled over your head. I haven't forgotten to write about you invincible saints who think you have a free pass to heaven. These are those of you who think God is your personal genie and yields to your every command as you believe that no one hears God better than you do. It's funny how these saints have a answer for everybody else's life without being able to see their own. How can you point your finger at everybody else's child while your children live like the devil in hell? Yep! I'm out there, I trust my Holy Ghost and I'm going to write until somebody gets delivered. Did the saved me become the kink in your armor? Shall unforgiveness separate you from the love of Christ? Rahab let's give them something to talk about! I show hope you didn't get your hair done before you got on the roller coaster named the quiet storm because there's a water fall up ahead and its sure to leave you drenched. It's time to get the actors out the pulpit. Yea, they're greedy dogs which can never have enough and they are Shepherds that cannot understand: they'll look to their own way, everyone for his gain, from his quarter. This is a Word to the Wise it's time to pray because the world has now crept into the church causing the church to become one big party full of Bible toting sinners who only want an association with God and not to submit to the power of God. Question. Have you ever asked God to cast out everything in you that's not like God? Do you have a hypocritical heart or an erroneous mind? The saved me has been talked about, criticized, used, abused and ostracized by you, you, you, you, you, and you and if I missed anyone then you too. My, my, my you wasn't even in my life testament but that demonic spirit that you need deliverance from landed you in A Word To The Wise. So on this day Rahab slinging dung let the pieces fall where they may and guess what she not ducking or hiding her hand. The same way the saved her is writing is the same way she'll preach it but with a little more stank on it. Don't you know she's a bonafide fighter? It's in her blood; she just don't fight the worldly way but she'll cut you quick spiritually. No she's not the tornado. She's the quiet storm spitting Word quicker than an m16 that's to all you gangster christians hoofing and puffing without power. My, my, my you tremble in those heels whenever I'm near but the saved me is not trying to hurt you I'm trying to help you before you burn in hell. Now what? You ready for me to stop? I haven't even got started yet I'm going to write until the tip of my pen pierce through the paper and my truth concerning you pricks your heart. Oh, you wonder if you can still be my friend? I don't play dirty, you've already been forgiven and the saved her loves you with the love of Jesus. But her pen is quick and sharper than a two-edge sword, dripping with the Word of God from its blade. (Moving right along) People of God a standard is a standard and that includes you Woman of God. It's not I don't wear finger nail polish but I get gel or acrylic nails with a french manicure with matching toes. How about I don't wear make-up, yet I have fake eye-lashes glued on. These are just a couple of things that make you go hmmm. How can you fix your mouth to talk about hair weave when you wear it? How can you talk about any woman being superficial in any manner when you yourself are guilty of the very same insecurity? I'm waiting because I just know you have a answer Mrs. Holier than thou my, my, my, my God today. Women of God if you have a standard how can you argue with the truth unless you reprobate? Let's talk about rhinestones from the perspective of someone who's visiting the House of God and looking in the pulpit asking this question. Why do you call that Woman of God worldly and untaught? Yet the Woman of

God with the rhinestone suit is called sanctified with a standard? One has on a pair of diamond earrings and a necklace with a matching bracelet. The other has on a suit with rhinestones around the collar, rhinestones around the wrist, rhinestones splattered across the suit jacket and rhinestones clear on down to the trim of the skirt, along with a rhinestone hat, rhinestone purse and matching rhinestone shoes. (You can straighten your wig now) Which Woman of God would you say is modest, the one with a few diamonds or the one with three-thousand? A stone is a stone whether it's a diamond or cut glass; we have a long way to go down on our knees; we must get back to the basics of holiness. People of God this is to all of you who've become hoodwinked and mesmerized by false prophets, as they bamboozle you, by preaching only what tickles your ears. While Satan has a noose around your neck and you can't even see that you're turning purple in the spirit. Why sit there and die? God wants to stop the hemorrhage of your suicidal lifestyle; can't you see your spiritual wrists are slit and nothing can save your life but Jesus. Don't you know sin lieth at the door and the punishment is more than you can bare? As you sit in the church house hand cuffed to the world living any kind of way. Guess what? You have no excuses for you've been warned and now your blind is open and everyone can see in. People of God dealing with the forces of evil are real; The saved her story allows you to see how she survived coming out of Satan's world and being birth into God's world. People of God as you navigate through the church a Word to the Wise has shined a light on how some church folk are bound by flesh, man and religious spirits. Preaching on sin is the type of preaching that when you hear it preached it pricks your heart just like it did mine and it will pull you out of the bowels of Satan. The saved her can write to you because she took a stand against the demonic forces of Satan and she became freed from multiple demonic spirits. The Power of God enabled her to tread over serpents and scorpions; she became the head and not the tail, her enemies have become her foot stool, no weapon formed against her shall ever prosper and her gift shall make room for her bringing her before great men. The power of the Holy Ghost has given her the ability to take authority over the enemy and to cast down imaginations and every high thing that exalted itself against the knowledge of God. She now has the power to bind and loose and she's blessed coming in and going out. (Hallelujah, Hallelujah, Hallelujah) This is why the saved her was so shocked to see the hypocrisy, the lack of integrity, lack of honesty and cruelty within the House of God but this is the conduct of those of you who need to be saved and delivered. So ask yourself am I saved and delivered? A Word To The Wise ask questions that you yourself may ask provoking the number one question. Do I truly have God or am I demonically influenced? The saved her is what she's become not of herself but through the Power of God and daily she ask God to send her some more forgiveness. People of God in these last and evil days God is gathering soldiers who can navigate through a colossal ring of pimping preachers, false prophets, self-righteous and religious spirits all who have an association with the seven deadly sins. (Pride, covetousness, lust, anger, gluttony, envy and sloth) This book is a warning (1 Peter 4:17) Judgment must first begin at the House of God. People of God it's time to re-examine yourself. Are you truly saved or are you fooling yourself? A Word to the Wise will give you an opportunity to heed the warning through this young Woman of God. If you've found yourself in this book that Rahab has written there's good news because you still have time right now to fall on your knees repent and seek yea the Lord while he may be found. For surely the day will come that some of you will call upon the name of Christ and he won't be there. People of God remember everything that's good to you is not good for you. So don't get caught eating out the hand of Satan when your number is called. People of God you should take heed because the Lord has told you all things. One of the darkest scriptures in the Bible (Jeremiah 8:20) The harvest has past the summer is ended and we are not saved. (Mark 13:20) And except the Lord shortened the days, no flesh should be saved. Heaven and earth shall pass away: but my words shall not pass away, I am Alpha and Omega, the beginning and the end, saith the Lord, which is, and which was, and which is to come, the Almighty. Wait until the roller coaster comes to a complete stop before exiting. I hope you enjoyed the quiet storm what a ride! Grace be with all them that love the Lord Jesus Christ in sincerity.

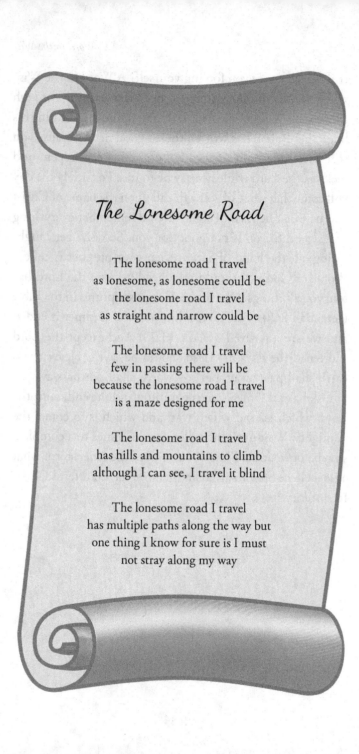

The Lonesome Road

The lonesome road I travel
as lonesome, as lonesome could be
the lonesome road I travel
as straight and narrow could be

The lonesome road I travel
few in passing there will be
because the lonesome road I travel
is a maze designed for me

The lonesome road I travel
has hills and mountains to climb
although I can see, I travel it blind

The lonesome road I travel
has multiple paths along the way but
one thing I know for sure is I must
not stray along my way

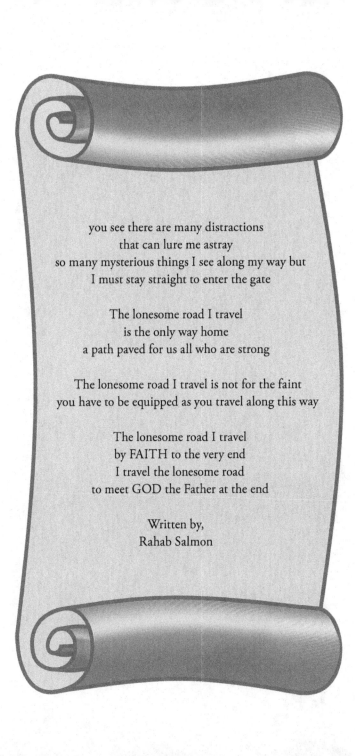

you see there are many distractions
that can lure me astray
so many mysterious things I see along my way but
I must stay straight to enter the gate

The lonesome road I travel
is the only way home
a path paved for us all who are strong

The lonesome road I travel is not for the faint
you have to be equipped as you travel along this way

The lonesome road I travel
by FAITH to the very end
I travel the lonesome road
to meet GOD the Father at the end

Written by,
Rahab Salmon

Printed in the United States
by Baker & Taylor Publisher Services